MW01155543

BUILDING AMERICA
THEN AND NOW

THE EISENHOWER
INTERSTATE SYSTEM

BUILDING AMERICA: THEN AND NOW

BUILDING AMERICA
THEN AND NOW

═┤ THE EISENHOWER ├═

INTERSTATE SYSTEM

JOHN MURPHY

CHELSEA HOUSE
PUBLISHERS
An imprint of Infobase Publishing

The Eisenhower Interstate System
Copyright © 2009 by Infobase Publishing

Chelsea House
An imprint of Infobase Publishing
132 West 31st Street
New York, NY 10001

Library of Congress Cataloging-in-Publication Data
Murphy, John, 1968–
    The Eisenhower interstate system / by John Murphy.
        p. cm. — (Building America : then and now)
    Includes bibliographical references and index.
    ISBN 978-1-60413-067-6 (hardcover)
    1. Interstate Highway System. 2. Roads—United States. I. Title.
    HE355.M87 2009
    388.1'220973—dc22   2008025544

Text design by Annie O'Donnell
Cover design by Ben Peterson

Printed in the United States

Bang FOF 10 9 8 7 6 5 4 3 2 1

This book is printed on acid-free paper.

CONTENTS

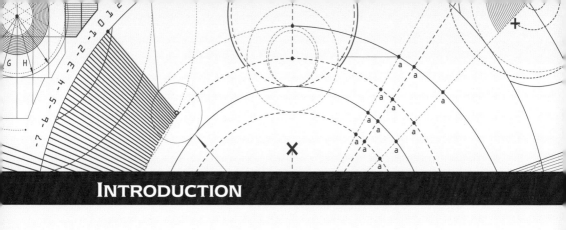

Uniting the States

Its total length is more than 45,000 miles; several of its 62 main streams flow uninterrupted for nearly 3,000 miles, while some of its 261 smaller tributaries run for fewer than 20. Its highest point reaches more than 11,000 feet above sea level, and its lowest dips 52 feet below sea level. It carries millions of tons of cargo and millions of human travelers every day. This massive and awe-inspiring network of streams and channels is not a mighty river but a human construction, one of only two human-made structures that astronauts have reported being able to see from space with the naked eye (the other is the Great Wall of China). This modern-day wonder of the world is the Dwight D. Eisenhower System of Interstate and Defense Highways, more commonly referred to as the Interstate Highway System.

Unlike most modern wonders and engineering feats, America's Interstate Highway System has enormous practical value to millions of people, not just those of a certain locality. In addition, it is as functional as it is visually impressive and mind-boggling in scale. Indeed, the vast majority of Americans—young and old—use the system every day of their lives, hitting the interstate highway to travel to the nearest city, to the supermarket, to work and school, to the airport or the stadium, to the movie theater and mall, or to their vacation destination. Rarely, if ever, in the history of human civilization have so many people enjoyed such an intimate familiarity with and access to an engineering marvel of this size and scope. It is not reserved for the ruling elite, a priestly class, or the honored dead, as are so many of history's wondrous constructions. Everyone is welcome to use the Interstate Highway System. It offers the promise of freedom and equality of access, security, safety, speed, and motion. In that sense, it is uniquely and distinctively American.

The vast network of superhighways, beltways, and spurs is a sort of ribbon that binds the United States together in an interconnected whole. As it traverses the distinctive and unique localities that make the United States such a dazzling mosaic of peoples and landscapes, the Interstate Highway System also imposes a kind of uniformity and standardization, providing travelers with a sense of continuity and familiarity even when far from home. The system enables a family from New Jersey to drive all the way to California, and it allows them to make this journey safely and quickly, remaining in a familiar comfort zone while still marveling at all the unfamiliar, unique, and sublime sites that make America so inspiring. The interstates knit all Americans together. Without them, the United States could very easily feel like—and become—the Untied States.

THE FIRST "NATIONAL ROAD"

The idea for a mighty national road that would traverse and unite the American states is as old as the nation itself. Soon after the end of the American Revolution, George Washington recognized the practical and cultural importance of a road that would serve as a "wide door" and a "smooth way" between the states.

Still vulnerable to the threats of the British and Spanish colonial powers that surrounded the 13 original states, the new nation

With firsthand experience of the poor roads crisscrossing the United States, President Dwight D. Eisenhower became determined to build a national system of highways. Referred to as the "Father of the Interstate System," Eisenhower successfully pushed Congress to fund the massive project.

required a passageway that would connect its vulnerable western settlers (in Ohio country) to the states east of the Appalachian Mountains. In addition to these concerns for defense and national unity, President Washington also viewed the proposed National Road as essential to the fledgling nation's economic vitality. Goods had to be able to flow smoothly and quickly throughout the states, especially the stream of raw materials from western frontier outposts to manufacturers in eastern cities. Many of the nation's roads—especially those that ran through the Appalachians to the western frontier—were little more than dirt trails. They meandered through nearly impenetrable forests and swamps, and quickly turned to mud or washed out altogether in storms.

Not until the nation's third presidency did the National Road begin to become a reality. In 1806, Thomas Jefferson authorized the project, and construction began in 1811. By 1839, the job was completed; the 600 miles of highway connected Baltimore, Maryland, to Vandalia, Illinois, just shy of the Mississippi River. The daunting and often impassable Appalachians were now much more readily traversed by a stone road, and the peoples of the new nation were more tightly connected in terms of security, defense, commerce, communication, and travel. As Washington had envisioned, the United States were now far more united.

IKE: AN INTERSTATE VISIONARY WITH A "GRAND PLAN"

Another man who recognized the crucial importance and national significance of a technologically advanced, uniform, safe, and efficient highway system was General Dwight D. ("Ike") Eisenhower, who was sworn in as president of the United States in 1953. Like George Washington, another president and former general, Eisenhower viewed an interstate "national road" system as vital to the national interest on several counts: defense, commerce, safety, and unity.

After much debate and wrangling with Congress and the individual states over funding, Eisenhower saw his "Grand Plan" begin to be realized. In June 1956, the Federal-Aid Highway Act was signed into law. By August, construction on the Interstate Highway System began in Missouri. Ultimately, there would be nearly 45,000 miles of wide and smoothly paved roadway organized into a grid of 35 north-south roads and 27 east-west highways, along with more than 260 beltways and spurs to serve urban areas.

CRITICISM AND UNFINISHED BUSINESS

Today, Eisenhower's Grand Plan has largely been realized, its goals met, and its vision fulfilled. The United States has an unparalleled highway system, in terms of size, scope, and complexity. Goods move efficiently and inexpensively. Drivers and passengers are statistically twice as safe on an interstate as they are on any other type of road. Year after year, interstates have served as vital and effective evacuation routes in advance of hurricanes and rising floodwaters. Even the Hurricane Katrina disaster would have been far worse had so many thousands of people not been able to drive away quickly from New Orleans when they were instructed to do so.

This is not to say that there are not problems with the system or that it enjoys universal acclaim. The Interstate Highway System has justifiably been blamed for furthering urban blight, environmental racism, environmental pollution and degradation, fossil fuel dependence, urban and suburban sprawl, homogenization of American landscapes and culture, and ongoing congestion. In addition, the system's future is clouded by debates over such issues as the introduction of tolls, privatization, infrastructure maintenance and safety, and responsible energy consumption.

THE INTERSTATES: UNIQUELY AMERICAN

The Interstate Highway System, at the same time a glorious triumph and a disappointing failure, will no doubt continue to evolve as the United States has. New engineering, vehicular, and materials technology; global environmental policy; and changing personal habits and lifestyles will force the system to adapt. What is certain is that the Interstate Highway System is an enduring marvel of conception, design, and construction. It is a daily testament to the genius and brawn of its planners and builders and, most of all, to its namesake and prime mover, Dwight D. Eisenhower. This is the epic story of its creation and the can-do American spirit of ambition, intelligence, and know-how that made this seemingly impossible wonder of the modern world possible.

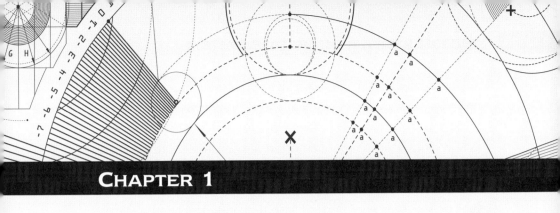

CHAPTER 1

The Good Road Movement

The freedom of movement and personal independence that Americans now cherish and consider their birthright was largely made possible by the invention of the automobile, a self-powered vehicle that made the crossing of great distances a far easier proposition. This new and curious invention was first made in Massachusetts, in the late 1890s, by two bicycle mechanic brothers from Springfield, Charles and Frank Duryea.

THE BIRTH OF THE AUTOMOBILE AGE

Meanwhile, in Detroit, Michigan, Henry Ford was working on a similar machine, mounting a two-cylinder engine on a carriage affixed with four bicycle wheels. This prototype vehicle was called the "Quadricycle," and it had neither brakes nor a reverse gear. Ford would follow the Duryea Brothers into the car manufacturing and sales business in 1903, offering his Model 999 car to the public. In 1908, he introduced his now-famous Model T (nicknamed the "Tin Lizzie"), which featured innovations that are now standard in all American cars, including a left-hand steering wheel and enclosed engine and transmission.

The easy affordability of Ford's cars encouraged people to take a chance on them; once these new customers drove their first automobiles, they could never go back to horse-drawn carriages. Car sales throughout the country took off, and half of all cars on the road were Fords. The automobile had been successfully introduced to the United States, and America's love affair with the open road was rekindled. It became ever more important, therefore, for the nation's roads to be upgraded to meet the new demands of America's burgeoning car culture.

One thing quickly became clear to all drivers of these new automobiles: America's roads were in terrible shape. A growing

Henry Ford's Model T *(above)* was the first affordable, mass-produced automobile. Credited for "putting America on wheels," the Model T quickly grew in popularity as ordinary folks were soon seen cranking the engines of their shiny new vehicles and driving off in a cloud of dust and fumes.

consensus emerged that something needed to be done about the shameful state of the nation's roads. Several years earlier, the League of American Wheelmen—a bicycle lobbying group—had already begun what became known as the Good Roads Movement. The league's founder openly criticized the current state of the roads and articulated a clear and compelling vision of a future more appropriate to America's greatness in the world. According to Tom Lewis's *Divided Highways*, the founder said that "American roads are among the worst in the civilized world and always have been . . . I hope to live to see the time when all over our land, our cities, towns, and villages shall be connected by as good roads as can be found."

The League of American Roadmen furthered the Good Roads Movement in its publication *Good Roads*, through its sponsorship of Good Roads associations and conventions, and by its political lobbying of state governments for road improvements. In 1891, these efforts began to pay off when New Jersey passed the first-ever road construction bill, pledging state aid to the infrastructure projects. In Cleveland, the league was instrumental in the inauguration of a series of paved test roads, designed to educate decision makers and the public at large about the enormous value—in terms of ease and economics, pleasure and safety—of travel along paved roads.

ROAD CENSUSES AND TEST ROADS

In 1894, a one-year federal study of national road conditions, road management, and construction techniques was funded. The nation's first-ever federal road agency, the Office of Road Inquiry, was created. It was an extremely modest operation. Yet the office's three employees applied themselves to the task at hand with the energy and resourcefulness of a federal agency 20 times their size—and they earned outsized results.

These three men, led by former Union general Roy Stone, launched a comprehensive federal survey of every single road in every single state. They had their work cut out for them. As Dan

McNichol points out in *The Roads That Built America*, "At this point, there wasn't a single accurate highway map of the United States. Not one person knew how many miles of highways the country had or where they lay." Counties were asked to identify each of their roads and to describe their conditions, including whether they were dirt or some harder surface. The Office of Road Inquiry devoted most of its tiny budget to setting up paved road demonstrations around the country. By building 21 segments of paved road only a few hundred feet long in nine states, General Stone hoped to get the regular citizens who test-drove on them so excited about the idea of good roads that they would convince their state and federal governments to fund and construct them.

FARMERS TO THE RESCUE

The Good Roads lobbyists and bicycle club members found and joined forces with a powerful new ally in their battle: American farmers. Because of the poor conditions of most roads, farmers were frequently frustrated in their efforts to get their livestock and produce to market. Wheel-sinking muddy roads, axle-busting potholes, and flood-obstructed stretches slowed farmers' progress from farm to market and back, and resulted in lost time, higher prices for their goods, and lower profits. They were fed up with the decrepit road system, especially in one of the most prosperous and technologically advanced nations of the world.

Paved test roads like those constructed in Cleveland and Boston caught their attention, and they immediately recognized the very real value of smooth, well-constructed roads. They saw how a paved roadway would result in substantial savings of time and money. Then, as now, American farmers could raise a powerful collective voice, one heard loud and clear by politicians in Washington, D.C. To ignore this raised voice would be to risk alienating the crucial sensibilities—and even more crucial votes—of the American heartland.

The test roads performed exactly as designed, both as effective demonstrations of the benefits of paved roadways and as a publicity and marketing tool. People did indeed get excited about the prospect of paved roads running throughout their towns, counties, and states.

MORE CARS, WORSE ROADS

The rising national excitement about—and the increasingly vocal demand for—paved roads coincided with the automobile's sudden explosion of popularity in the United States. In the six-year period between 1906 and 1912, the number of cars owned by Americans leapt from 108,000 to 944,000. According to Tom Lewis's *Divided Highways*, by 1921 there were 9 million automobiles on the road, and by 1929 that number increased to 26.5 million. As cited by Mark H. Rose in *Interstate: Express Highway Politics, 1939–1989*, a survey conducted by the General Federation of Women's Clubs in the late 1920s revealed that just over half (55.7 percent) of American families owned a car, and almost one in five of those families (18 percent) owned more than one.

Thanks largely to Henry Ford's mass production of affordable cars, the automobile was quickly shedding its status as a luxury or novelty item and becoming an everyday tool for average Americans who used it to get to work, perform errands, haul produce and goods, and travel. In addition, trucks began to carry and deliver more and more goods interstate, biting into and undercutting the long-haul business long monopolized by the railroad industry. They gained an advantage over the once mighty railroad barons by offering competitive hauling prices, more convenient routes, and more flexible schedules.

Even as Americans got behind the wheel in ever-growing numbers, however, the roads only continued to deteriorate. Several years after its study began, the Office of Road Inquiry published its national road census findings. The results were astonishing, even to those people who were all too familiar with the mud-soaked, potholed, bumpy ride that characterized

The popularity of the Model T allowed people to travel farther and faster than ever before, encouraging them to visit new places. A new federal agency was soon created to collect information on the safety and quality of the nation's roads and highways. Road improvements decreased transportation times and even made the national parks accessible to motorists. *Above*, inspectors on the Yellowstone Trail, 1914.

the American driving experience. Though the United States had more than 3 million miles of roadway spreading across its length and breadth, only about 350,000 miles of these were paved in some fashion. That meant that roughly 9 of 10 American roads were dirt—more often than not, they were mud. Drivers generally were kept to speeds below 25 miles per hour by the poor road conditions. In addition, road maintenance was rarely if ever performed in any regular, organized, or expert manner.

The number of automobiles and trucks soon hit a critical mass, and local, state, and federal governments realized that they had to take action to create a safer and more reliable network of roadways. They were helped along in this decision by the ongoing lobbying efforts of farmers, railroaders, road builders, construction material suppliers, tire makers, gas station owners, and ordinary automobile owners and drivers, all of whom had some stake—economic and/or personal—in better and safer road construction and maintenance.

THE FEDERAL-AID ROAD ACT OF 1916

All of this lobbying from numerous interested parties eventually forced the various levels of government to pay attention to the state of the nation's roads and to seek a solution to the pervasive problems. At long last, federal funds were devoted to road improvement and construction, complementing similar state efforts. Over the years, the funds made available rose in rough proportion to the boom in automobile usage (from $75 million spread across five years in 1916, to $75 million annually beginning in 1921, to $750 million a year by 1929). The very first federal roads bill, the Federal-Aid Road Act, was signed into law by President Woodrow Wilson in 1916.

The Federal-Aid Road Act created a new federal agency called the Bureau of Public Roads and provided it with a budget of $75 million. This money was to be dispersed to the states within five years, but a state would receive its share of the money only if it had formed a dedicated highway department. At this point, one out of four states did not have its own highway department. In addition, each state was expected to match the amount of money it received from the federal government. This meant that, if the Bureau of Public Roads gave a state $2 million to help pay for road construction, repair, and maintenance, the state would be required to raise and spend the same amount on its roads.

This was to be a federal-state partnership, not a mere handout from Washington. The states were forced to take an active supervisory interest in the health and safety of their own roads. In fact, the states would have the power to decide which roads

Bumpy, rough, and muddy when wet, many of the country's roads hindered motorists, cyclists, and others from traveling or transporting their goods. These conditions forced the government to pass the Federal-Aid Road Act, a bill that funded the construction of paved roads *(above)*.

they wished to improve and where they would like to construct new roads. They would also have the right and responsibility to manage and maintain the roads. The federal government provided funding but otherwise largely stayed out of the states' way in terms of decision making, day-to-day operations, and management.

A SLOW START

Despite the clamor for good roads that had been building for years, the first few years that followed the signing of the Federal-Aid Road Act were marked by sluggish inaction. States were slow to develop their highway departments. Some failed to create sufficient matching funds. The Bureau of Public Roads had dispersed only half a million of its $75 million budget. Cooperation between state officials, local builders, and federal engineers was poor. Coordination between states and counties was also lacking, so that relatively few stretches of new paved road crossed state or county lines and extended beyond them, resulting in a lack of comprehensive and extensive road improvements. Some politicians and Good Roads advocates instead began to float alternate proposals for the building of several federally planned, constructed, and owned cross-country highways, cutting out the states' involvement altogether. Many of the people who proposed this course of action believed that the states' role—up to this point—was characterized mainly by mismanagement, poor and illogical planning, inefficiency, and obstructionist tendencies.

Most dispiriting of all, only 12.5 miles of new paved road had been constructed by 1919. This disappointing progress could not be ascribed entirely to state or federal foot-dragging. The United States' involvement in World War I began in 1917, the year after the roads bill was signed into law. Materials, resources, engineers, and manpower were redirected either to the armed forces or into wartime industry. Domestic infrastructure projects were largely put on hold until the war's end. Worsening an already bad situation, the roads actually deteriorated further under the pounding they received by wartime convoys of tens of thousands of heavy trucks that carried materials and supplies from the heartland to eastern ports, where they met Europe-bound cargo ships.

American roads needed a champion and a savior. They would get both in the figure of Thomas Harris MacDonald.

CHAPTER 2

Thomas MacDonald and the Bureau of Public Roads

Following the end of World War I and the stateside return of American manpower, expertise, and resources, the road construction movement regained its lost energy and momentum and again became a national priority. The man who would lead this charge for 34 years was Thomas Harris MacDonald, former chief engineer of Iowa's highway commission. In this position, he ordered and oversaw the regular grading, stabilizing, smoothing, and paving of thousands of miles of Iowa roadways. This drastic improvement in state road conditions resulted in the highest ownership of automobiles per capita in Iowa than in any other state at the time.

MacDonald knew how to get results, and he knew how to improve, build, and maintain roads. His road-building skills and dramatic success in Iowa got the attention of bureaucrats in Washington who were trying to figure out how to fulfill—and kick-start—the stalled mandate of the 1916 Federal-Aid Road Act. In 1919, during Woodrow Wilson's presidency and a year after the end of World War I, MacDonald was chosen by U.S.

While serving as a highway engineer for the state of Iowa, Thomas Harris MacDonald (above) was hired to collect road data for the federal government, earning one dollar a year for his work. Eight years later, MacDonald was promoted to chief of the Federal Bureau of Public Roads. In that position, he increased road construction, educated the public about highways, and lobbied for increased federal spending in transportation.

Secretary of Agriculture David Houston to serve as head of the Federal Bureau of Public Roads (previously the Office of Road Inquiry, the small agency that launched the national roads survey in 1894 and got the federal ball rolling on the better roads movement).

MacDonald, generally referred to with both fear and respect as the "Chief," quickly sized up the nature and extent of the morass in which the road improvement initiative had become mired. He was one of the first federal officials to envision a cohesive nationwide network of interstate highways that featured state-of-the-art engineering. He immediately swung into action to get the process back on track and moving again. Echoing the thoughts of George Washington before him, and anticipating those of Dwight D. Eisenhower after him, MacDonald began his reconception of the national road improvement project by identifying the four main purposes that would be served through the creation of a sound nationwide system of paved roadways: strengthening of national defense, improving economic welfare of farmers, boosting intra- and interstate commerce, and encouraging Americans' freedom and safety of movement.

BUILDING ALLIANCES

MacDonald realized that these four purposes incorporated a wide range of interest groups and potential beneficiaries. He sought to breathe new life into the large and unlikely alliance of individuals, automobile touring associations, construction materials manufacturers, contractors, and representatives of the automobile, oil, insurance, steel, rubber, and road-building industries. Their combined demands had previously resulted in the 1894 creation of the Office of Road Inquiry (predecessor to MacDonald's Bureau of Public Roads) and the passing of the 1916 Federal-Aid Road Act.

To this large group of parties that possessed a stake in improved roads, MacDonald added state highway associations and their officials. This was the Chief's attempt to both expand the range of voices that demanded action on roadway construction and improvement and to mend the federal-state relationship—a partnership that had frayed in the years since the Federal-Aid Road Act had gone into effect. One of the primary ways in which he brought state highway officials into the fold was to tap into the American Association of State Highway Officials (AASHO), a preexisting group that was founded in 1914. He encouraged members of this group to cultivate relationships

BUILDING AMERICA NOW

SEEING MORE CLEARLY

The green backgrounds and white lettering that have been a trademark feature of interstate highway signage since its first evaluation on a test road in Greenbelt, Maryland, in the late 1950s are about to undergo a subtle but significant change. The letter font in use since the dawn of the interstate era has been something called "Highway Gothic." Although the letters are legible in daytime conditions, when headlights shine on this chunky typeface at night, the letters tend to "bloom," blur, and glow, decreasing their legibility—especially for the increasing number of elderly drivers on the highways. Two graphic and type designers named Don Meeker and James Montalbano have created a new highway font they call "Clearview." Its letters are cleaner, lighter, thinner, and therefore less prone to blurring and fuzziness when illuminated by bright light.

After several years of lobbying the Federal Highway Administration to switch to their font, Meeker and Montalbano finally convinced federal highway officials in 2004 to allow states to use it on all of their road signs. More than 20 states have already adopted the typeface and are using it to replace existing signs as they wear out.

with their state's congressional representatives and senators and to lobby them directly on all matters that pertained to road building and improvement.

Another important alliance MacDonald forged in his effort to build a modern national road system was between his office and the U.S. armed forces. Pitching his belief that good roads were crucial to national defense, MacDonald sought all the help the military could give in terms of materials, information, and expertise. He found a very receptive audience. The armed forces, having endured the slowgoing misery of American roadways during the military convoys of World War I, were eager to see upgrades to the system of highways crucial to their deployment of men and equipment during wartime and other times of national emergency.

MacDonald persuaded the military to part with more than $100 million worth of surplus equipment—including trucks, steam shovels, and hand shovels—free of charge. He also worked closely with General John J. Pershing, the U.S. Army's War Plans Division, and the Geological Survey to create a map of interstate routes that General Pershing considered vital not only to military mobilizations and national security but also to commerce, industrial growth, and the daily needs of ordinary citizens. The "Pershing Map" is considered the first formal and articulated plan for a modern interstate highway system, and it would later provide President Eisenhower with a solid framework upon which he could construct his own vision for an interstate network of superhighways.

Perhaps most importantly, MacDonald did not overlook his most vital resource and valuable constituents: ordinary American citizens. The average American might not be a farmer, a worker in the road-building trades, an auto industry employee, or a member of an automobile touring association. Yet, increasingly, the average American was an automobile owner and user. MacDonald made sure to inform this growing majority of citizens about what was at stake and how they personally stood to benefit from better roads. He created a Highway Education Board to publish pamphlets, booklets, and informational films that were sent to schools, civic organizations, and local chambers of commerce. He also sent speakers throughout the country to address these groups and to teach students, businesspeople, homemakers, and other "ordinary" Americans the very real value of safe, smooth, efficient roads and highways. In addition, MacDonald's Bureau of Public Roads published a monthly journal entitled *Public Roads: A Journal of Highway Research*, to which the Chief himself frequently contributed writing.

Public Roads usually featured extensive research data collected by the Bureau of Public Roads. One of MacDonald's great passions was research and data collection. He encouraged members of his office and state officials to compile as much information as possible to determine where new roads were most needed, which older roads should be repaired and upgraded, what materials should be used, how strong various pavement types were, what prevailing traffic patterns were, how regularly maintenance would be performed on any given stretch of roadway, and how that would be undertaken. MacDonald even studied traffic signs, including the shapes, colors, and lettering that drew the eye most effectively and resulted in the greatest clarity and legibility, thereby increasing road safety.

AN ALL-AMERICAN JOB

This intensive effort, coordinated lobbying, and partnership building began to pay off for MacDonald and for the nation's roads. After only two years as head of the Bureau of Public Roads, MacDonald had increased the total length of newly paved roadway from 12.5 miles to 5,000 miles, and more than three times as many miles were under construction. Not content to rest on his laurels or ease the pressure that he and his Good Roads coalition had been applying on the federal government, MacDonald successfully demanded and received a highway spending bill that greatly increased his office's budget and the funds available for new road construction. The Federal-Aid Highway Act of 1921 authorized the spending of $75 million a year on the nation's roads (with the states again providing matching funds), a 500 percent increase in spending over the 1916 Federal-Aid Road Act.

GETTING YOUR KICKS ON ROUTE 66

Perhaps the most famous pre-interstate federal-aid highway was the legendary Route 66 (officially known as U.S. 66), which ran almost 2,500 miles, all the way from Chicago, Illinois, to Los Angeles, California, and passed through Missouri, Kansas, Oklahoma, Texas, New Mexico, and Arizona.

The highway became the main western route to California taken by migrant farm families during the Dust Bowl years of the Great Depression. John Steinbeck, in his novel based on this mass migration entitled *The Grapes of Wrath,* immortalized the highway and referred to it as the "Mother Road," for the hope with which the westward road filled these starving, despairing Americans. Route 66 was further celebrated in a song written by the jazz musician Bobby Troup entitled "(Get Your Kicks) On Route 66," made popular by the singer and pianist Nat "King" Cole. The "kicks" referred to were the dazzling and delirious roadside attractions and "tourist traps" that proliferated along the route's length, including reptile museums, exotic animal farms, neon signs, roadside sculptures, diners that offered giant steaks and "blue plate specials" (usually a low-priced meal of meat and several kinds of vegetables), theme motels, Indian trading posts, filling stations, and the world's first McDonald's fast-food restaurant—not to mention the natural beauty of the quintessentially American landscape it passed through, particularly in the Southwest.

With the advent of the interstate age, however, Route 66 began to die. Stretches of interstate highway ran parallel to the old Route 66, whereas other portions of the new highways integrated the old

Just as significant as its generous funding was the new Highway Act's formalization of the partnership between the federal and state governments that MacDonald had fostered and sought to repair. Without a functioning, healthy partnership of this kind—based on mutual respect and trust—very few roads would

Route 66 (*above*) was the first paved road connecting the Midwest to the Pacific coast. Before the national interstate system was finished, rural farmers often used Route 66 to distribute their crops, while others used the road for travel, causing a boost in regional tourism.

route. By 1970, most of Route 66 had been either absorbed or made obsolete by interstate highways, and the tourist attractions (and many towns and businesses) along its length simply disappeared. In 1985, the old highway was decommissioned by the American Association of State Highway Officials, and a great American institution passed into the mists of legend.

get past the planning stage, little would get built, and much time and money would be wasted for scant results. From that point on, instead of building isolated stretches of paved road that did not connect across borders with similar highways of neighboring states, each state would design at least 7 percent of its new or repaired roadways to link up with the paved roads of other states. The Bureau of Public Roads and state highway departments would work together to identify and operate these routes as federal interstate roads. This burgeoning network of paved roads would pass through the county seats of each state before they connected to similar roads in neighboring states, eventually creating a truly national highway system that satisfied both intra- and interstate driving and hauling needs.

MacDonald had received the federal resources and commitment he sought, and his vision was quickly becoming a reality. According to Tom Lewis, MacDonald said, "My aim is this: We will be able to drive out of any county seat in the United States at thirty-five miles an hour and drive into any other county seat—and never crack a spring." Elsewhere, according to Dan McNichol, MacDonald pithily summed up both the grandness of the project and the sheer grit and resolve it would take to accomplish it, exclaiming, "This is an All-American job!" Indeed, he believed that the national road-building project was every bit as important an undertaking and as vital to national interests as was the transcontinental railroad 50 years earlier. MacDonald also correctly predicted that his extensive, densely webbed highway network would largely supplant the railroad system, since it would be able to carry people and goods to more places, more quickly and flexibly, with greater freedom of choice and mobility.

ESTABLISHING UNIFORM STANDARDS

One of MacDonald's main goals was to impose some logic and clarity on the nation's network of roads. Until this point, America's highways had developed in a random, haphazard, casual fashion. Approximately 450 interstate highways and "trails" ran throughout the country, but they were poorly mapped, if at all, and were often poorly supervised and maintained by "trail associations." One or more trail associations would adopt over-lapping stretches of roadway, so a single road would be known by several names. Signage, if it existed at all, varied widely in quality, accuracy, and consistency from trail to trail.

MacDonald was determined to hack through this thick tangle of trails and impose a grid-like network of interstate highways. Working in close consultation with the states' representatives from the AASHO, MacDonald instituted the now-familiar route numbering system, which replaced legendary road names such as the Dixie Highway, the Lincoln Highway, the Yellowstone Trail, the Leatherstocking Trail, the Ethan Allen Trail, and the National Road. North-south routes were now assigned odd numbers, starting with 1 on the eastern seaboard and ending with 101 along the Pacific Coast. East-west routes received even numbers, starting with 2 running along the northern tier of states and with 70 along the nation's southern borders. Major north-south interstate routes would end with a 1 or a 5. Major east-west transcontinental routes would end with a 0.

MacDonald and the state officials from AASHO also settled on uniform shapes for interstate road signs: a black-and-white shield with the state name, below which would appear "U.S." and the route number. They also designed black-bordered, bright yellow octagonal (eight-sided) danger and stop signs and diamond-shaped caution signs (such as Slow, Curve Ahead, Road Narrows, etc.). Speed-limit signs would have black letters and borders against a white background. Before this, there was no standardization of road signs state to state or even county to county, a fact that explains much of the confusion and difficulty people experienced on America's roadways. Getting from point A to point B before the MacDonald era often meant getting hopelessly lost, with no reliable map to save the day. As Dan McNichol points out in *The Roads That Built America*, poor and

In order to create a simple system of route signs, Thomas Harris MacDonald designed a series of symbols and numbers that would replace long and inefficient names. This system allows travelers to easily determine what road they are on and where they are going by route number and the shape of the sign *(above)*.

inconsistent signage probably was a major contributor to the nation's shockingly high annual toll of traffic fatalities as well: 20,000 a year by the mid-1920s.

MacDonald's desire to create a rational, uniform, efficient network of interstate roads was being satisfied, and at a blistering pace. Gone was the sullen sluggishness that had characterized state construction efforts following the passage of the 1916 highway funding bill. Indeed, by the end of the 1920s, more than 90,000 miles of roadway had been built or upgraded and paved. Between the beginning of 1927 and the end of 1929, almost 80,000 miles of road were built or repaved. The federal government was spending more than $75 million a year on road construction, and, collectively, the states kicked in even more.

MacDonald believed this federal-state effort represented one of the three great highway building projects in all of recorded history, on par with the monumental roads projects of the Roman Empire and Napoleon Bonaparte. The Chief was now something of an imperial ruler himself, holding together and ruling over an unwieldy empire of builders, contractors, building material manufacturers, state highway officials, federal bureaucrats, and local, state, and federal politicians. Thomas MacDonald had become the emperor of the new American highway.

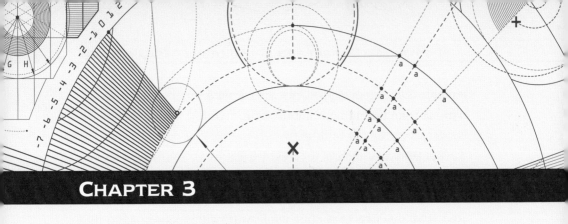

CHAPTER 3

The New Deal and Interstate Highways

Thomas MacDonald had been at the helm of the Bureau of Public Roads for a decade. Within that time he had successfully engineered a dramatic modernization and expansion of the nation's roadways and an equally radical overhaul of governmental attitudes regarding the political, economic, strategic, and social value of road building. In only 10 years, he had built almost 100,000 miles of paved highway, all while forging a strong and enduring federal-state partnership and liberating average Americans to hit the open road and go where they liked, when they liked, with a far greater degree of safety and confidence than they had before the Chief's reign began.

Yet, MacDonald felt his work had only just begun, and he looked forward to extending the growing network of American roads throughout the coming decade of the 1930s. Just as World War I had idled the United States' first road-building push, however, a new calamity arrived at the end of the Roaring Twenties to dampen America's high spirits and plummet the nation into a prolonged economic crisis that threatened to halt MacDonald's army of road builders in their tracks.

THE COUNTRY CRASHES, BUT AMERICA CONTINUES TO BUILD

With the stock market crash of October 29, 1929, the United States was ushered into a severe, worldwide, decade-long economic downturn known as the Great Depression. Just as the nation was emerging as one of the wealthiest, most technologically advanced world powers in the wake of World War I, its growth was abruptly stunted. Money was suddenly scarce, poverty spread, and many Americans lost their jobs and began to go hungry. At the height of the Depression in 1933, almost one-fourth of the American workforce was unemployed.

The country appeared to be sliding away from the glittering technological promise of the twentieth century, and all the prosperity, ease, and wonder it seemed to have once offered. Instead, gaunt, unemployed Americans were living in tent cities, selling apples on Wall Street, and driving thousands of miles to California to pick grapes for pennies a day. The interstate highways that had symbolized boundless freedom and opportunity just a year before were now grim refugee trails that led hungry families toward desperate migrant worker encampments and backbreaking labor.

Changed in spirit as they suddenly seemed, these interstate roads would not be neglected during the Depression as they had been during World War I. MacDonald continued to lobby for highway funds and argue for the ongoing national importance of road building and maintenance, especially with so many Americans suddenly crisscrossing the country in desperate search of work. The value of interstate highway construction as an engine for both employment and economic activity was not lost on MacDonald or on state and federal politicians. So, while cash and funding dried up throughout much of the country, highway spending actually increased, and quite dramatically. During his final term in office, President Woodrow Wilson increased annual federal spending on highways from $75 million to $125 million and budgeted for an additional $80 million to be used in the future.

The funding floodgates would really open under Franklin D. Roosevelt, affectionately known as FDR. President Roosevelt was a strong believer in the importance of public works projects to keep Americans employed and to spur activity that would spark an economic revival throughout the country. His extensive package of spending, work, and relief projects was collectively known as the New Deal, and it is generally credited with helping to drag the United States out of its economic doldrums and to boost the drooping American morale in the process.

Far from viewing his programs as mere make-work projects or desperate attempts to spend his way out of the Depression, Roosevelt believed he was providing idled, scared, and traumatized Americans with honest work of very real value. In addition to putting Americans back on the job, Roosevelt intended to have them create public works of lasting practical and symbolic value—enduring monuments to American grit, determination, know-how, and craftsmanship. MacDonald's emerging network of interstate roads meshed perfectly with Roosevelt's vision of a busily employed citizen workforce laboring on a project that would be both a symbol of undiminished American greatness and ambition and a public resource of enormous practical and daily utility.

Though he was initially skeptical that road building would spur much economic activity and kept highway funding at levels set by the Wilson administration, Roosevelt gradually came around to the idea, particularly as the national unemployment figures grew worse and worse. Quite suddenly, MacDonald saw the highway budget leap from $125 million a year to several hundred million dollars annually (more than $250 million a year on average, a doubling of the previous highway budget under President Wilson). Between 1933 and 1940, Roosevelt allocated just under $2 billion

During the Great Depression, many people who lost their homes and jobs were forced to live in shantytowns known as Hoovervilles. In an effort to provide job opportunities for the poor, President Franklin D. Roosevelt poured money into government projects, including the federal interstate system. *Above*, the largest Hooverville in New York was located in an empty reservoir in Central Park.

for road construction and improvement (accountings of federal spending on roads during this period can vary widely, partly due to the complicated nature of New Deal agencies and their funding; some commentators cite a figure of $1 billion, whereas others report $2.8 billion or more). This massive infusion of cash, along with the sad fact of the sudden availability of cheap American labor, allowed MacDonald to greatly expand his network of federally funded roads to 225,000 miles by the mid-1930s. Even then, the Chief refused to ease up; he added 12,000 paved miles to the system every year for the next decade and a half.

Roosevelt was pleased with the results MacDonald achieved in creating an interstate network of paved roads that, after some twisting and turning, would connect the East Coast with the West Coast through a series of separate but connected roadways. MacDonald had dramatically transformed the American transportation landscape, laying hundreds of thousands of miles of paved road and highway along with clear, consistent signage and rational route layouts, where—just a decade before—there had been little more than mud, potholes, and mass confusion. Yet Roosevelt had something even more ambitious in mind.

FDR'S VISION FOR AN INTERSTATE HIGHWAY SYSTEM

In February 1938, FDR summoned MacDonald to the White House. Spread before him was a map of the United States upon which he began to draw six lines. Three of these lines ran north to south, from the Canadian border to the southern extremities of the nation, and the other three ran east to west, from coast to coast. He explained to MacDonald that these lines represented a new network of transcontinental toll highways that he proposed. Rather than the usual two-lane highways that MacDonald had been building, Roosevelt wanted these new interstates to be "superhighways": wide four-lane expressways free of the frequent stop signs, traffic lights, town and city intersections, and railroad crossings that slowed and bunched the traffic that increasingly congested MacDonald's roadways.

In some ways, though MacDonald's federal-aid highways were still under construction, they were already becoming obsolete: More and more drivers clogged the roads, many of them wishing to bypass villages, towns, and cities altogether and simply drive long distances unimpeded by any slowdowns and interruptions. In addition, truck traffic was increasing dramatically, as the railroads lost more and more freight-hauling business to the rapidly growing trucking industry. Roosevelt had the foresight to recognize this and proposed a smaller system of roads designed especially for those drivers and commercial truckers who wished to travel vast distances quickly—with a minimum of stopping and sightseeing or puttering around local communities—and who were willing to pay for the convenience. FDR envisioned a two-tiered system of national roads: long, broad, continuous superhighways that carried people across the country in a hurry, and the narrower, slower intra- and interstate highways that suited more local business, Sunday driving, sightseeing, and shorter visits to neighboring counties and states.

Before their meeting was over, Roosevelt, fully aware of MacDonald's passion for research and data collection, asked the Chief to study the question and report back to him on the desirability and practicality of his superhighway plan. MacDonald did so within only two months. According to Richard F. Weingroff in his article "Essential to the National Interest," MacDonald concluded in his written report to the president that "a national system of direct route highways designed for continuous flow of motor traffic, with all cross traffic on separated grades, is seriously needed and should be undertaken." As part of the Federal-Aid Highway Act of 1938, Roosevelt asked MacDonald to undertake another feasibility survey and study of national traffic patterns and emerging needs—one that would help address congressional concerns and questions, and, hopefully, convince representatives and senators of the need for the new network of superhighways.

Fiercely independent and bent on protecting the autonomy of his Bureau of Public Roads, MacDonald did not bow to Roosevelt's considerable power and charisma. The Chief did not provide the president with the conclusions he hoped for. In his report, submitted to FDR and Congress in April 1939 and entitled "Toll Roads and Free Roads," MacDonald stated that Roosevelt's vision of a network of four-lane transcontinental superhighways was possible but not advisable. Because MacDonald's exhaustive research had shown that most traffic in the United States centered in and around cities, the Chief found no justification for

Elected during an economic crisis, Franklin D. Roosevelt *(above)* became responsible for rebuilding the country's financial institutions and helping ordinary citizens find jobs and homes. He quickly realized the federal interstate system could provide jobs to millions of poor citizens and worked with Thomas MacDonald to expand the project.

a massive building project that would traverse primarily rural areas. Only a very small percentage of drivers and truckers on any given day were engaged in a cross-country journey. MacDonald crunched various economic statistics regarding automobile ownership, family income, fuel prices, and other factors and concluded that not enough American drivers would be willing to pay tolls—a relatively rare idea and practice in the 1930s—to fully fund the construction, maintenance, and operation of the superhighway system.

Yet MacDonald did share some portion of Roosevelt's vision, and he acknowledged that the existing interstate highways were becoming increasingly congested, especially in cities and surrounding metropolitan areas. In addition, as the winds of war again began to blow and the nation was being dragged into World War II, the highways' role in national defense and safety again became an issue. Suddenly, the possibility of rapid mobilizations of troops and evacuations of citizens from one regional population center to another became of paramount importance. So, in a follow-up report entitled "Interregional Highways" (1941), MacDonald counterproposed a more modest but targeted solution to the growing urban traffic problems—which included a stalled flow of cars going into and out of cities and clogging downtown streets—and the national need for rapid, high-volume interregional links. In his report to FDR and Congress, MacDonald outlined a new series of interregional roads, stretches of four-lane highways that led into and out of cities, and large expressways that ran straight through cities.

Congress agreed with MacDonald's proposals, and—eventually and reluctantly—so did a disappointed Roosevelt. The Federal-Aid Highway Act of 1944 mandated the upgrading and construction of a "National System of Interstate Highways" that comprised 40,000 miles of roadway, to be planned and built under the direction of MacDonald and the Bureau of Public Roads. MacDonald set aside more than 5,000 of those miles for city expressways and metropolitan feeder roads (approaches that flowed into and out of urban areas). According to the Department of Transportation's article "Dwight D. Eisenhower National System of Interstate and Defense Highways," the act summarized the project's goals as the construction of a network of highways "so located, as to connect by routes, direct as practical, the

THE PENNSYLVANIA TURNPIKE

Work on the Pennsylvania Turnpike began in October 1938, and the new superhighway officially opened less than two years later, on October 1, 1940. The turnpike was an immediate success. Motorists in far greater numbers than expected proved more than willing to pay for the luxury of driving fast on a wide, smooth, uninterrupted modern highway. Yet, despite the large number of drivers, highway safety increased dramatically on the turnpike; road fatalities were reduced by the absence of railroad crossings, dangerous intersections, and collisions with other vehicles crossing the road.

Income from toll collections also exceeded expectations and eventually made the new superhighway profitable, even after maintenance costs were deducted. Tolls were initially to be collected only until the bonds were paid off, but Pennsylvania found it hard to deny itself such a large and tempting source of income. Drivers also demonstrated a continued willingness to pay for the convenience and relative safety of the superhighway, so tolls became a permanent feature of the turnpike.

Other states took notice of Pennsylvania's success, and—within a few years of the Pennsylvania Turnpike's opening—many of them made plans for their own turnpikes. Maine, New Hampshire, New Jersey, Ohio, Indiana, Kansas, West Virginia, and New York all created turnpike authorities and began ambitious superhighway projects. They also sought to link up their new highways as much as possible. As a result, in the words of Tom Lewis, "By 1955, a driver could travel from New York to Chicago over superhighways without ever encountering a stoplight."

principal metropolitan areas, cities, and industrial centers, to serve the National Defense, and to connect at suitable points, routes of continental importance in the Dominion of Canada and the Republic of Mexico."

TURNPIKES TAKE CENTER STAGE

Thomas MacDonald won the battle against a national system of transcontinental toll roads, but his influence began to wane because of his opposition to tolls, highway privatization, and new superhighway building through rural areas. As progress on building the Chief's own National System of Interstate Highways—really just a series of urban expressways and suburban commuter highways into and out of cities—stalled and traffic problems worsened, more and more states began to clamor for superhighways that would run through their territories and connect them with the rest of the nation. Individual states began to seize the initiative and did not wait for federal planning, approval, or funding. They formed their own turnpike authorities and planned toll highways that would service not only the cities and their circling suburbs but also those rural regions MacDonald felt were unnecessary to traverse with high-speed, high-volume roadways.

Pennsylvania was the first state to plan and build its own turnpike, a road that drivers pay to use. Unlike the kinds of highways that MacDonald had been building for almost 30 years—one lane of paved roadway in each direction, with stop signs, traffic lights, city and town intersections, and railroad crossings—this would be a superhighway with higher speed limits, two lanes going in each direction, and an uninterrupted drive that would slice through cities or pass around or over them. To reach city streets, towns, villages, or other destinations off the turnpike, drivers would exit and get onto smaller highways and local roads. The turnpike itself would be designed for motorists driving long distances at high speeds who were not interested in making a lot of stops along the way.

Although Thomas MacDonald, the chief of the Federal Bureau of Public Roads, was not in favor of building large highways in rural areas, state governments took it upon themselves to start their own projects. The Pennsylvania State Turnpike *(above)* was constructed with financing from several of President Roosevelt's New Deal agencies. Highly publicized and successful, Pennsylvania's new four-lane superhighway inspired other states to build their own turnpikes.

Bonds sold by the state government would pay for the turnpike's construction costs. Pennsylvania eventually convinced Roosevelt to buy the bulk of these bonds through the Public Works Administration and the Reconstruction Finance Corporation, two of his New Deal agencies. MacDonald's Bureau of Public Roads was not involved in the financing, planning, or construction of the Pennsylvania Turnpike. Watching major road-building projects from the sidelines was an entirely new and unpleasant sensation for MacDonald, but one that he would have to get used to.

In these circumstances, the Bureau of Public Roads was becoming increasingly irrelevant and idle. In the postwar years, as state turnpike authorities rose to prominence and increasingly took over highway building, MacDonald began to be left behind and was less often consulted on road matters. By the time Dwight D. Eisenhower—the U.S. general and supreme commander of the Allied forces in Europe during World War II—rose to the presidency in 1953, MacDonald realized that his own time had passed.

After 34 years and more than 3 million miles of paved highway, Thomas MacDonald had reached the end of the road. The Chief had transformed America's roads and interstate highway system and, as a result, had immeasurably improved the nation's commerce, defense, daily commutes, and recreation and travel opportunities. Yet the time had come for the Chief to leave his office and yield to the vision of another great American roads enthusiast, one who came into the office of the presidency with a "Grand Plan" for the nation's highway system.

CHAPTER 4

Eisenhower's Grand Plan

Like George Washington—another general and president—Dwight D. Eisenhower's appreciation for the value of smooth and dependable national roads stemmed from his wartime experiences. As a lieutenant colonel in the army following the end of World War I, Eisenhower had participated in a unique and dramatic demonstration organized by his superiors.

THE 1919 CONVOY

During World War I, the army endured innumerable logistical difficulties, mechanical disruptions, and schedule delays in moving troops, supplies, and military material due to horrible road conditions. As a result, they wished to call the public's and politicians' attention to the problem. If another large-scale conflict broke out, or if foreign invaders attacked the United States, the national road network would have to become a far more reliable and efficient means of moving citizens, troops, and military machinery. This was no longer merely a cause for recreational motorists and car and bicycle clubs. This was now a pressing national defense issue. To graphically illustrate to Americans the size and scale of the problem, the army organized a convoy of military vehicles to travel a 3,000-mile journey from the White House lawn to San Francisco, California, in July and August 1919.

The convoy of 81 vehicles—trucks, ambulances, cars, motorcycles, mobile dining and kitchen cars, and boat and artillery hitches—was three miles long from front to rear. It labored its way at an average of five miles an hour on roads made of sand, mud, and dirt through 11 states and 350 cities. Sometimes the convoy could manage to move only three miles in an entire day. It took two months for the convoy to complete a trip that would take less than a week today. As bad as the roads were before the army launched its attention-getting demonstration, they were considerably worse after the convoy rumbled through. Almost a hundred bridges were damaged or destroyed by the weight and pounding of the heavy military vehicles. Already deeply rutted roads were torn up even more. The convoy itself suffered, too. More than 10 percent of the vehicles were abandoned along the way, rendered inoperable by the punishing road conditions.

As arduous as this cross-country expedition was, the army convoy made its point quite clearly. Officers and soldiers met ordinary citizens all along the route who pleaded for better roads. The terrible road conditions that the enlisted men experienced temporarily were ordinary Americans' daily reality, and they were fed up with it. The officers, who were in a position to make recommendations to their superiors, were shocked, dismayed, and—quite literally—rattled by what they experienced.

The United States could not hope to fulfill its emerging role as a leading world military power with such a crude and backward system of national roads. Lieutenant Colonel Eisenhower, in particular, took extensive notes on the road conditions he experienced, including routes, building materials, construction techniques, and road design. The publicity the convoy attracted and the public debate it sparked dovetailed with the Good Roads lobbying movement of the time and helped gain passage of the Federal-Aid Highway Act of 1921, which increased the budget for road building and repair by 500 percent.

EUROPEAN HIGHWAYS AND WORLD WAR II

In general, western European roads and highways were superior to those in America, a fact that was further brought home to Eisenhower during World War II. Now a general in the army and supreme commander of all Allied forces in Europe, Eisenhower quickly recognized the value of the dry, paved roads that ran throughout France and Germany. Having established a foothold in Normandy, France, Eisenhower began ferrying troops, supplies, and artillery through France to meet the enemy forces of Nazi Germany. After the Allies had bombed and destroyed much of France's railroad, to prevent its use by Germany as a supply chain or troop mobilizer, Eisenhower moved quickly to seize control of French roads.

Once he did so, Eisenhower ordered the rapid conversion of several hundred miles of road to a sort of superhighway network, including a divided highway that ran directly from Normandy to Paris. The general then established the "Red Ball Express," a fleet of about 6,000 army trucks that plied the highways 24 hours a day, constantly hauling supplies to Paris. Eisenhower even set up gas and service stations (staffed by mechanics and tow truck drivers), rest areas (with food, toilets, and sleeping accommodations), and military highway patrols all along the route. Once Paris was secured and the Germans were on the run, another Red Ball superhighway was fashioned from existing French roads. This highway provided the Allies with a high-speed route between Paris and the new front lines in Germany.

When American soldiers (including General Eisenhower himself) invaded Germany, they were astounded by the country's main highway: the legendary autobahn. It was built for the very same reasons that George Washington and Thomas Jefferson's National Road, MacDonald's network of national highways and interregional expressways, and Eisenhower's Interstate Highway System were built—to create jobs, to spur commerce and boost the economy, to unify the country, to link the nation's cities, and to open up uninhabited territory to tourists and settlers. The autobahn was almost 2,500 miles long when World War II interrupted its construction. It was designed to be nearly 4,000 miles long. The autobahn was entirely paved—with two lanes that ran in each direction, uninterrupted by stop lights or train

As a lieutenant colonel in the U.S. Army, Dwight D. Eisenhower witnessed firsthand the terrible state of the country's roads while serving with the War Department's First Transcontinental Motor Convoy (above). Hampered by impassable roads and vehicle damage, the entire expedition took two months to complete and convinced the federal government to fund a massive road improvement project.

crossings—and it featured a complex series of ramps and over-passes designed to separate military and civilian vehicles when necessary. To an American army that was accustomed to crawling at five miles an hour over rutted dirt and sliding mud roads that were poorly mapped (if at all), the autobahn's smooth surface, engineering marvels, and 100-mile-per-hour speeds were like a science fiction vision of the improbable future.

Once the Allied forces under Eisenhower gained control of the autobahn, they used it to move rapidly throughout Germany, chasing the Germans ever deeper into their own country and away from the European territory they had violently conquered years earlier. Control of the autobahn allowed the Allies to maintain efficient supply lines and to funnel ample provisions, materials, and rested troops (who were not used to traveling in such relative ease) into Germany, even as German troops grew increasingly weary, hungry, and exhausted. Germany quickly surrendered following the Allied invasion, a success due in no small measure to Eisenhower's Red Ball Express.

By war's end, Eisenhower had become a passionate believer in superhighways. In his memoirs, quoted by both Tom Lewis and Dan McNichol, the general who later became president would recall, "After seeing the Autobahns of modern Germany and knowing the asset those highways were to the Germans, I decided, as President, to put an emphasis on this kind of road building. This was one of the things I felt deeply about, and I made a personal and absolute decision to see that the nation would benefit by it. The old convoy had started me thinking about good, two-lane highways, but Germany had made me see the wisdom of broader ribbons across the land."

Dwight D. Eisenhower would not be elected president of the United States until 1952; however, in the years between the end of World War II and his inauguration, Eisenhower never let go of his dream to build an American autobahn. Immediately after he entered the Oval Office, he began plotting how best to craft a proposal to Congress and the 50 states for a state-of-the-art national network of interstate superhighways.

SUBURBANIZATION AND DETERIORATION

In many important respects, American roads actually deteriorated following World War II, despite the dawn of a new boomtime era of postwar American prosperity and expansion. The economy was humming: American industry reverted to peacetime activity, and American families—long deprived by wartime shortages and rationing—enthusiastically spent money on new homes and big-ticket consumer items, including cars and houses in the suburbs. The postwar years, and the hope and prosperity they inspired, resulted in a prolonged "baby boom" that greatly swelled the nation's population and the size of the average American family.

Before the war, the majority of Americans lived in cities, often in close proximity to—if not in the same apartment as—their extended families, including siblings, aunts, uncles, cousins, and grandparents. The general availability of automobiles, the increase in paved highways that led into and out of cities, the growing size of American families, and the sudden need to find housing for newly returned soldiers all contributed to growing suburbanization throughout the country. As the American economy became oriented less toward heavy industry and more toward retail services and white-collar industries (such as advertising, insurance, and banking), companies and stores often joined the growing exodus to the suburbs.

Soon, more and more of people's work, leisure, and family time was spent in the suburbs. While suburban growth exploded, the roadways that serviced them and connected them to the cities (where the majority of breadwinners still worked) were not upgraded accordingly. Cars were getting bigger and bigger, and every year there were more of them on the stressed roads, but the highways were still relatively old (on average, their surfaces were

12 years old), narrow (as little as 20 feet wide), two-lane black-tops. In the immediate postwar years, Thomas MacDonald and his Bureau of Public Roads had been able to upgrade less than 6,500 miles of the 40,000 miles that the Federal-Aid Highway Act of 1944 had mandated.

MacDonald—who was always committed to research, statistics, and clear-eyed acceptance of facts over issues of pride or ego—admitted his bureau's failure when he released the results of its own study, which concluded that almost 8 of 10 American roads were overused or in unacceptably (and dangerously) poor condition. Quite simply, MacDonald's treacherously narrow and increasingly degraded interstates could no longer handle the growing number of large, fast cars that traveled greater distances outside of and between major urban areas.

NEW IDEAS CROWD OUT THE OLD CHIEF

President Eisenhower's emerging vision for America's network of highways would differ markedly from MacDonald's interstates. First, Eisenhower planned to pay for the new interstate highway network through the charging of tolls. This approach, known as self-liquidating funding, would allow Eisenhower to build ambitiously and spend liberally—he initially proposed to spend $50 billion. This wildly expensive building project would not affect his budget at all; he wouldn't have to spend a single federal dime on the highway system. The tolls would be repealed after the highways were fully paid for (a similar promise regarding Pennsylvania Turnpike tolls was quietly broken; the turnpike remains a toll road to this day, approximately 70 years after it opened). MacDonald strongly opposed user fees for highways and the reliance on private ownership or operation of turnpikes. He believed that roads should remain public and therefore be funded publicly, using government money. He also believed that private operation or ownership of roads usually resulted in maximum profit-taking and minimum reinvestment in the roads in the form of necessary repairs, maintenance, and upgrades.

Eisenhower had also concluded that the interstate super-highways he envisioned would have to be built essentially from scratch. He decided that most of MacDonald's highways were unsalvageable for his purposes; they could not be easily upgraded, widened, or rerouted. Instead, he imagined his superhighways running alongside the older interstates, which would now operate in the shadow of these massive, towering, high-speed, uninterrupted, transcontinental expressways. They would be "limited access" highways, meaning they could be entered and exited only at a relatively small number of designated points. There would be no intersections, stop signs, or traffic lights.

The older federal-aid highways would be reduced to a mere shadow of their former selves, serving mainly as feeder roads to the superhighways or as local "scenic" routes that often ran roughly parallel to the superhighways. In Eisenhower's conception, the new superhighways were to connect cities but not pass through them. Instead, older expressways and beltways would channel city-bound highway traffic into and out of urban areas, preventing congestion on the new interstates. The additional land needed to build the new interstates—both the ground beneath them and the "right-of-way" on either side of the roadbed—would necessitate federal seizure of state and private property, a process known as eminent domain.

MacDonald found little in this new highway scheme to interest or please him. In turn, Eisenhower decided that MacDonald was no longer the man for the job. Soon after Eisenhower took office, the new president sought and received the Chief's resignation. Thomas MacDonald had taken America far down the road toward highway modernization and safety. He had laid the foundation for Eisenhower's system of superhighways and had provided him with a partial blueprint to follow. Yet MacDonald had gone as far as he could go, and his vision of road building had stalled, overtaken by shifting social patterns, technological advances, and the changing needs of an increasingly mobile and suburban citizenry. It was time to yield to a new group of highway enthusiasts and engineers who would continue his excellent work and usher the United States into its greatest era of highway building, an ambitious period of colossal construction, engineering genius, and political will unparalleled to this day. At the heart of this new era, and providing its lifeblood, was President Eisenhower's "Grand Plan."

APPEALING TO THE NATIONAL INTEREST

President Eisenhower decided to forge ahead and take his plan directly to state governors. He figured he could use the opportunity afforded by the July 1954 Governors' Conference to at least broach the subject and get the debate rolling. He was not interested in ramming his scheme down anyone's throat. Instead, he simply hoped to present his vision for a national interstate highway system and to get the governors and state highway officials talking and thinking about how they would like to see the project designed and implemented.

Given that many commentators and historians believe the Interstate Highway System was one of the legislative proposals closest to Eisenhower's heart throughout his two terms as president, it is a sad irony that he could not articulate his vision in person. The president was forced to change his schedule following the death of his sister-in-law, so Vice President Richard M. Nixon was sent to deliver Eisenhower's proposal to the state governors instead. Nixon (himself a future president)—never known for his inspiring rhetorical skills or comfort as a public speaker—read directly from Eisenhower's notes. Even so, he quickly got the attention of the governors who sat before him.

Eisenhower proposed a Grand Plan: a 10-year, $50 billion road-building and improvement project that, according to Tom Lewis in *Divided Highways* and Richard F. Weingroff in his article "Essential to the National Interest," would feature federal-state cooperation, state control of roads, and long-sought solutions for "the problems of speedy, safe, transcontinental travel— intercity communication—access highways—and farm-to-farm movement—metropolitan area congestion—bottlenecks—and parking." Eisenhower did not spell out how the $50 billion would be raised or by whom. Instead, he asked the governors to put their heads together and submit to Congress their funding proposals.

Fifty billion dollars was an almost unfathomable amount to spend on a project, especially by a president who belonged to the traditionally anti–big government Republican Party. It could either be a windfall to the states or a crushing burden, depending on who ended up paying the bill and how the costs would be shared. Eisenhower headed off potential skepticism by assuring the governors of the cooperative nature of the planning and building. This would be a true "cooperative alliance," in his words.

What truly excited and inspired the governors was the sheer breadth and ambition of the Grand Plan. As Richard F. Weingroff, information liaison officer in the Federal Highway Administration's Office of Infrastructure, points out, most people today mistakenly believe that Eisenhower was proposing only the Interstate Highway System. In fact, his plan was far grander than that. The new interstate highways were merely one component of a comprehensive effort on the federal, state, county, city, and town levels to improve and upgrade all of the nation's roads. Technologically advanced interstate and transcontinental superhighways served as the project's glittering centerpiece, but the modernization of more humble state highways, county routes, and local roads would be of equal importance and value to the national interest.

It was this appeal to the national interest that got the attention of average Americans, who were often wary of big government spending projects and make-work programs. Annual highway deaths numbered in the tens of thousands (more than 36,000 a year), while injuries numbered 1.3 million per year—casualty figures that rivaled those of wartime. Lawsuits over car accidents and road-related automobile damages clogged the courts. The costs of these casualties and related lawsuits totaled more than $4 billion annually. Americans were collectively spending billions of hours in traffic jams, which resulted in the loss of billions of dollars due to wasted productivity. Though American industrial productivity and efficiency skyrocketed in the postwar years, these gains were frittered away by the difficulty trucks experienced in delivering goods to markets and to ports. These difficulties resulted in delays, which translated into $5 billion worth of extra shipping costs passed on to consumers in the form of higher retail prices.

Finally, though America felt strong and prosperous to an unprecedented degree following World War II, it also felt haunted and vulnerable in ways far more profound than ever before. The end of World War II ushered in the atomic age, and the world's only other remaining superpower, the Soviet Union, had thousands of nuclear missiles trained on U.S. targets 24 hours a day. Americans feared, on a daily basis, a devastating nuclear attack.

Given the extreme tensions and poor diplomatic communication that characterized Cold War relations between the United States and the Soviet Union, these fears were not at all unjustified. If such a nuclear attack came to pass, the affected areas would need to be evacuated quickly before radiation sickness felled large numbers of civilians. In addition, the armed forces would need to transport thousands of soldiers and millions of tons of equipment to stricken areas, strategic hot spots, or locations vulnerable to post-nuclear invasion. The current national system of roads—interstate highways, state highways, and county routes alike—were not up to this task, having been largely neglected since Roosevelt's prewar administration. Indeed, according to Weingroff in his article "Original Intent: Purpose of the Interstate System, 1954–1956," Eisenhower's notes for the Governors' Conference bewailed the "appalling inadequacies [of the current national interstate road network] to meet the demands of catastrophe or defense, should an atomic war come."

Having appealed to the governors—and, by extension, the public at large—on the grounds of safety, congestion on

Built during Adolf Hitler's rise to power and World War II, the German autobahn *(above)* is an extensive national network of roadways that provided the inspiration for President Eisenhower's interstate system. Using 80,000 workers, the Nazis constructed 3,000 miles of the autobahn in less than five years—one of the fastest road construction projects in history.

the roads and in the courts, economic health, improved commerce, and national defense and security, Eisenhower echoed many of the sentiments of George Washington, not to mention those of Thomas MacDonald when he took over as chief of the Bureau of Public Roads in 1919. Like Washington and MacDonald, Eisenhower's appeal on these grounds was successful, though the eventual results would be hard won and many years in the making.

Eisenhower's statement, which issued a final challenge to the governors to study his proposal and report back to him with suggestions to put it into action, ended by placing the ball in the states' court, while at the same time indicating that this new and upgraded national road network would be built. The states either could take shared ownership of the network, or they could get out of Eisenhower's way. The former general was determined to see his Grand Plan become a concrete reality.

THE CLAY COMMITTEE

Eisenhower did not want any momentum to be lost while the state governors debated his scheme and hashed out competing schemes for its realization, so he attempted to both frame his proposal and solve its nagging problems by forming two exploratory committees. Collectively, they were designed to address the main concerns associated with the project: how to build the interstates, how to justify and sell the plan to the public, and, most importantly, how to pay for it. The Interagency Committee, led by Francis du Pont, would solicit the input of officials from the defense, treasury, and commerce departments, as well as representatives of the president's Council of Economic Advisers and the Budget Bureau. This committee would study the issue of how to fund Eisenhower's highway plan.

The other committee—the president's Advisory Committee on a National Highway Program—comprised a select handful of prominent engineering, construction, and machine equipment industrialists, bankers, and union leaders. It was led by Lucius Clay, a former general and engineer who had served under Eisenhower in Europe during World War II, where he helped devise and implement Allied supply line systems. He was also a major figure in the planning and execution of the postwar Berlin airlift (a humanitarian delivery of food, fuel, and other basic supplies to West Berlin following the Soviet blockade of the city in 1948). Logistical planning was his strong suit, and Eisenhower needed Clay's analytical mind applied to the thorny and stubborn problems of the Grand Plan. Indeed, the committee became commonly known as the Clay Committee, a testament to the former general's influence and intellect.

The Clay Committee relied on research compiled by du Pont and his deputy Francis Turner. A thorough and tireless researcher and analyst, Turner proved so valuable to the Clay Committee that he was eventually appointed its executive secretary. The House and Senate came to rely on his expertise and insight while grappling with Eisenhower's plan and crafting legislation to flesh it out. The nation's governors also came to lean heavily on Turner. Following the Governors' Conference, the state leaders had formed their own committee to study and respond to Eisenhower's highway plan. This was named the Special Highway Committee, and their deliberations were based mainly on funding estimates and cost projections provided by Turner and the Bureau of Public Roads.

THE GOVERNORS RESPOND

In December 1954, after almost six months of study, the nation's governors submitted their response to Eisenhower's plan. In its conclusions and broad outlines, it strongly echoed the president's rationales for an urgent and ambitious cooperative national highway-building project. Their counterproposal, entitled "A Cooperative Program for Highway Construction," noted the nation's substantial growth in both population and economic activity. Yet it rang the same alarm bell that Eisenhower did, warning that the nation's roads were not currently capable of accommodating this growth. The national road system's inadequacy would result in lost economic opportunities, reduced growth, and increasingly treacherous driving conditions.

Although the cost of constructing and upgrading a new national road system would be undeniably high, the costs of the current inadequate road network were estimated to be as much as $3 billion a year due to injuries, deaths, work time lost to traffic jams, and difficulties and delays in transporting commercial goods. Statistics provided by Francis Turner and the Bureau of Public Roads had made it clear to the governors that one of every seven American workers used highways to get to and from work or had a job that relied in some way on daily highway use. In addition, one of every six businesses that sold retail or wholesale goods (such as clothing, food, appliances, and automobiles) and services (such as restaurants, gas stations, mechanics, and trucking companies) were located along highways and/or depended on highways and motor vehicles to conduct their operations.

The governors acknowledged that although they, with the help of Bureau of Public Roads statistics, were only now coming to grips with the extent of the problems on the nation's roads, ordinary American drivers had long been familiar with the system's ills. As quoted by Weingroff in "Original Intent":

> The inadequacy of our present network of highways is a matter of common knowledge. Traffic jams, insufficient parking space, frequent detours, and worn-out surfaces serve the motoring public as indices of the situation, just as traffic counts, sufficiency analyses, accident rates, transportation costs, and other technical indices serve the expert. In spite of record expenditures for highways, the situation has reached a critical stage.

The governors' bottom-line response to this growing crisis was a proposed 20-year highway construction effort and a doubling of current annual spending on roads (from $47 billion to more than $100 billion). They neglected to make any concrete proposals regarding exactly how to raise the funds for the project, but they made it clear that they wanted the federal government to pay the bulk of the bill, in partnership with the states. The current federal-state roads funding formula was a 60/40 setup, with the federal government providing 60 percent of the funding for federal-aid highways. The governors hoped a similar arrangement could be achieved to build the new interstates. Responding to President Eisenhower's Grand Plan for a comprehensive network of interconnected national, state, and local roads, the governors proposed a three-tiered system of highways: the new interstate superhighways; the older, preexisting federal-aid interregional highways built by Thomas MacDonald; and state and local routes.

The governors' proposal, largely an endorsement of Eisenhower's vision, signaled the states' enthusiasm for the project and willingness to share its burdens and responsibilities. The nagging question of funding was left unresolved, but the president had gained the cooperation and support of the very leaders who could have created insurmountable roadblocks to his Grand Plan.

FUNDING DEBATES

While the governors' Special Highway Committee studied the issue, the Clay Committee sought ways to make Eisenhower's ambitious scheme a reality. It submitted its own report in January 1954, one month after Eisenhower received the governors' proposal.

A parade of lobbying groups—which represented road builders, pavers, contractors, concrete and rubber suppliers, automobile manufacturers and dealers, trucking associations, petroleum producers and sellers, state highway officials, motorist clubs, and ordinary private citizens—quickly convinced the committee of the need for the interstates and an integrated national road system, and of the economic opportunities the project would present, both in its building phases and when in full operation. In addition, both American industry and the American people had clearly signaled their strong desire to see this project succeed. Selling the idea to the public was not going to be a problem after all.

Once the question of whether to build the interstates and how to rationalize it to the public was settled, the Clay Committee turned its attention to the far thornier matter of funding. Everyone who came before and wrote to the committee expressed a strong desire for Eisenhower's interstate highways. No one, however, expressed an equally strong willingness to shell out for it. Opinions and suggestions varied widely. Some believed that all American taxpayers should foot the bill because the interstate system was designed as a national defense network. Others believed that a gas tax should fund the project, forcing drivers to shoulder the burden of the road building that would primarily benefit them. Similarly, some people felt that the interstates should be operated as toll roads, thereby ensuring that only highway users, rather than the general public, would pay for their construction and upkeep. Still others argued that even nondrivers would benefit from the new road network, since a vibrant economy and lower consumer prices (a result of lower shipping costs and greater efficiency) were good for every American. Therefore, all Americans should be asked to contribute to the funding through a general tax of some sort; the easiest solution would be to funnel a portion of every American's income tax toward a highway construction fund.

Clay and his fellow committee members ignored all of this advice and came up with their own funding strategy. They had concluded that the Interstate Highway System would cost a total of $27 billion over a 10-year period of construction ($23 billion for the interstates themselves, and $4 billion for feeder and distribution routes that would connect the interstates to cities they passed near and through). The total budget for the creation of an integrated national system of interstate superhighways, interregional highways, state and county routes, and local roads would be $101 billion. In addition to the $23 billion to be spent on the interstates, $30 billion would be spent on primary highways (interregional highways and urban expressways, beltways, bypasses, and feeder roads), $15 billion on secondary highways (rural routes), and $33 billion on other roads and streets in cities, towns, villages, and rural communities. This enormous sum of money would be raised by the selling of bonds. The preexisting gas tax and other "user taxes" would pay off these bonds over time. Tolls would be charged in only a few instances. The federal government would be responsible for 90 percent of the interstate's construction costs, and the states would contribute the remainder. With regard to the primary and secondary highways, and the other roads slated to be built or upgraded as part of the project, the federal government would be responsible for about a third of the funds; state and local governments would provide the rest. Planning and construction would be achieved through federal-state cooperation. Taxes would not rise, and no new taxes would have to be created. The federal deficit would not be increased by a single dollar.

On paper, it sounded like a reasonable and prudent plan, and one unlikely to raise the hackles of taxpayers, state governments, federal officials, or special interest groups. To buttress its proposal and justify the huge expenditures, the Clay Committee appended the following celebration of America's automobile age with a dire warning and punctuated it with a stirring challenge, as quoted in Weingroff's "Original Intent":

> We are indeed a nation on wheels and we cannot permit these wheels to slow down. . . . We have been able to disperse our factories, our stores, our people; in short, to create a revolution in living habits. Our cities have spread into suburbs, dependent on the automobile for their existence. The automobile has restored a way of life in which the individual may live in a friendly neighborhood, it has brought city and country closer together, it has made us one country and a united people. But America continues to grow. Our highway plant must similarly grow if we are to maintain and increase our standard of living. . . . In fact, we face a challenge today and America has ever evidenced its readiness to meet a challenge head on with practical bold measures.

Despite this rock-solid reasoning—and the appeal to patriotism and the traditional American can-do spirit—the Clay Committee's proposal, endorsed by Eisenhower and submitted to Congress in February 1955, would spark great controversy and ultimately die an untimely death. Yet, out of its ashes arose a consensus-driven highway bill that satisfied the president and set in motion one of the greatest building projects and engineering marvels in the history of the world.

CONGRESSIONAL WRANGLING

The Clay Committee proposal, officially titled "A Ten-Year National Highway Program," was forwarded to Congress with a letter written by President Eisenhower himself. In it, he repeated most of his arguments in favor of the project made to the Governors' Conference the previous summer. He cited the alarming highway casualty statistics, increasing traffic jams and poor road conditions, lost productivity, higher shipping costs and retail prices, and the need for a national system of superhighways that would provide for rapid mobilization of troops and evacuation of civilians in the event of nuclear war or other catastrophe. According to Weingroff in "Original Intent," Eisenhower introduced the Clay Committee report with an appeal to patriotism shadowed by gloomy predictions that echoed those in the report itself:

> Our unity as a nation is sustained by free communication of thought and by easy transportation of people and goods. The ceaseless flow of information throughout the Republic is matched by individual and commercial movement over a vast system of interconnected highways crisscrossing the country and joining at our national borders with friendly neighbors to the north and south. Together, the united forces of our communication and transportation systems are dynamic elements in the very name we bear—United States. Without them, we would be a mere alliance of many separate parts.

If the current "inadequate" highway system was not expanded, upgraded, and more thoroughly interconnected, this all-important commercial movement and communication flow would be disrupted, the country would splinter into an unwieldy and disconnected collection of regions and localities, and national unity would be shattered. The nation's crumbling road infrastructure was groaning under the weight of a critical mass of automobile traffic: In 1954, 48 million cars, 10 million trucks, and a quarter million buses were jammed up on 3,348,000 miles of deteriorating roads and streets. Unless something was done quickly, a tipping point approached in which massive gridlock and horrific accidents would cripple the nation and make it vulnerable to economic collapse and foreign attack. A modern and safe highway system was of the utmost urgency and demanded a prompt and positive response from Congress, Eisenhower concluded.

President Eisenhower's vision for the national interstate system was very different from that of Thomas Harris MacDonald, the chief of the Federal Bureau of Public Roads. By replacing MacDonald with General Lucius D. Clay and the Clay Committee *(above)*, Eisenhower ensured the new superhighway would be constructed to his specifications.

Despite the urgings of Eisenhower, the Clay Committee, and the state governors, the congressional reaction was far from positive—though it was fairly prompt. By this time, few members of Congress failed to recognize the need for a modern national highway system. Their constituents, who included powerful business interests, had clamored for just such a project for years. Yet, few of these congressional representatives wanted their home states to pay too high a share of the bill (if any) or to be responsible for running up the federal deficit. Opposition to the Clay Committee's bond-financing scheme arose immediately. Several senators were troubled by the fact that the federal government would pay interest to those people who bought the bonds to fund the highway project. Although this technically did not count against the federal deficit, many senators suspected it was a form of smoke-and-mirrors accounting. The money devoted to interest payments would also be unavailable for construction costs.

Alternative funding ideas began to be discussed. One proposal called for toll highways, in which tolls would be collected until the project was fully paid off. Others proposed the creation of a highway-building fund into which gas taxes would be deposited. To avoid debt spending, highway work would begin only when sufficient funds had been raised. Meanwhile, trucking and petroleum special interests—passionate proponents of Eisenhower's interstate system—lobbied hard against any increases in fuel taxes to pay for it. Truck and bus companies fought against new taxes on equipment or tires that would apply to them. Conversely, the American Automobile Association (AAA)—which represented average, noncommercial automobile drivers—argued for higher diesel, truck, and bus-related taxes, urging no increases on gasoline taxes that would affect ordinary car drivers.

Out of this riot of competing voices and a growing stalemate, House and Senate highway bills somehow emerged. The House bill, sponsored by Maryland representative George Hyde Fallon and based on a Senate version put forth by Tennessee senator Albert Arnold Gore (father of former vice president Al Gore, Jr.), called for highway construction through 1968. The project would be funded by the creation of a Highway Trust Fund, which would be supported by federal gas and oil taxes. Gas taxes would be raised a penny a gallon, and oil taxes would rise two cents a gallon. Similar tax increases would be applied to trucks, buses, trailers, tires, and engine oils. The federal government would assume about 90 percent of the construction costs, and the states were to pick up the rest. Congress would provide funding in stages and would disperse new funds only after the Bureau of Public Roads issued satisfactory status reports. Separate funding would be made available for interstate maintenance, including resurfacing, restoration, and rehabilitation of roadways and the reconstruction of bridges, overpasses, and interchanges. The combination of funding via the collection of user taxes and the release of funds in installments made this a "pay as you go" plan that, it was hoped, would appeal to those congressmen who were leery of huge federal spending projects and massive deficits.

A vote on Fallon's bill was held in late July 1955. It was defeated soundly, fatally wounded by the aversion to higher taxes shared by nearly all highway-related special interest groups, ordinary drivers, average citizens, and the timid politicians who fielded their angry calls and opened their poison-pen letters.

RISING FROM THE ASHES

All sides retreated to their various corners, licked their wounds, regrouped, and considered their options. In September 1955, President Eisenhower suffered a major heart attack and remained ailing—with this and other health problems—for most of the following 12 months.

During this time of enforced idleness and contemplation, Eisenhower wrote extensively in his diary and became increasingly anxious about what America would look like without a modern highway system. He foresaw a grim future of economic stagnation, increased highway carnage, and vulnerability to nuclear and natural catastrophe. His commitment to the interstate system was only strengthened during this difficult period of anguished reflection, and his sense of urgency greatly increased. So intense was Eisenhower's desire to see the interstates built that he began to consider alternatives to his bond-funding scheme. According to Mark H. Rose in *Interstate: Expressway Highway Politics, 1939–1989*, Eisenhower "just wanted the job done" and was willing to compromise on its funding.

BUILDING AMERICA NOW

NEW HIGHWAY TECHNOLOGIES

It used to be that interstate roadways, after they were cleared, plotted, dug, paved, painted, installed with signs, and opened to drivers, were simply left to the ravages of time and travel until the wear and tear became so great that lanes had to be closed and repaired. Today, however, the Federal Highway Administration has offered millions of dollars in grants to companies developing highway technologies that will result in safer and more durable roads.

Many of these companies are working on techniques that result in stronger and more reliable asphalt. One company studies technology that alerts road builders to possible weaknesses in pavement mixes that can be corrected before those mixes are poured onto road surfaces. Other companies work on sensors that determine the exact moment when asphalt sets properly and on early warning indicators that alert engineers to the possibility of temperature-related cracks. Even the lines painted on top of the asphalt are high tech, with tests now performed on highly reflective pavement markings than can be seen more clearly in rainy conditions.

Meanwhile, the various special interest groups who would most benefit from construction of the interstate system—truck and bus companies, road-building and materials industries, the automobile industry, oil and gas companies—began to accept the reality that a minor tax hike was a small price to pay for a modern, extensive, reliable, and interconnected network of national roads that would provide a major spur to their enterprises and greatly increase their revenues.

In this shifting climate, small modifications and significant compromises made a breakthrough possible in 1956. Eisenhower, Gore, and Fallon all reintroduced their previous year's bills with few, if any, alterations. The only significant changes were the increased collective will to get a highway bill passed and the new willingness to look beyond personal reservations.

Fallon's House bill called for a federal Highway Trust Fund to be created by fuel, vehicle, and other road-user taxes that would reimburse states 90 percent of the construction costs of 41,000 miles of uniform highway built to the highest standards. (In 1968, new legislation increased the interstate system's mileage to 42,500 miles. It also allowed any highway that met all interstate standards and was a logical addition or connection to the interstate network to be designated as part of the system.) Some tolls would be charged along certain stretches of interstate. The new interstates would receive $25 billion in funding, with primary and secondary highways receiving about $75 billion.

The Interstate Highway System was scheduled to be completed by 1972 and designed to accommodate the volume of traffic projected for 1975. Fallon's bill was passed by the House and Senate (with additions by Senator Gore) in April and May 1956 and was then sent to the White House.

CHANGING THE FACE OF AMERICA

Having missed out on the opportunity to introduce his Grand Plan to the Governors' Conference—and the nation at large—in 1954, Eisenhower was once again denied the chance to revel in

General Lucius D. Clay *(left)* and President Eisenhower *(right)* worked together in Europe during World War II and were close colleagues. When Eisenhower needed someone to help him build an interstate system, Clay rose to the challenge to assess the needs and requirements of the project.

a crucial developmental stage of his most important presidential initiative. Still recovering from his heart attack and receiving postoperative care for an intestinal infection, the president was forced to sign his long-sought highway bill from his hospital room in the Walter Reed Army Medical Center, two years to the month after Vice President Nixon delivered Eisenhower's proposal to the state governors. With no witnesses to the historic moment other than his press secretary, James C. Hagerty, Eisenhower declared himself to be "highly pleased"—surely a monumental understatement given his many years spent working toward this goal and the preceding months of extreme anxiety about its future.

The passage of the Federal-Aid Highway Act of 1956 into law positioned Eisenhower's vision to become a reality. He had won the "pay as you go," self-financing highway system he had long argued for, without saddling the nation with the burden of a crushing federal deficit. Most importantly, he had ensured that the nation would receive the modern, interconnected, trans-continental highway system it deserved as a world superpower and required if it hoped to continue to safeguard its prosperity, safety, security, and very future.

The National System of Interstate and Defense Highways began construction within one month, and in only three months the first eight-mile section was completed, in Eisenhower's home state of Kansas. Even Eisenhower—who had led the invasion of Normandy on D-Day, brought Nazi Germany to its knees, and had become the leader of the mightiest nation of the free world—seemed awed by what was about to be accomplished, as he later recollected in his memoir (according to both McNichol and Weingroff):

> More than any single action by the government since the end of the war, this one would change the face of America. . . . Its impact on the American economy—the jobs it would produce in manufacturing and construction, the rural areas it would open up—was beyond calculation.

Tom Lewis, in his book *Divided Highways*, spells out exactly how awe inspiring and monumental this project—which we now take completely for granted—really was:

> The task the highway officials faced was Herculean: Build 41,000 miles of divided, limited-access highways to rigorous specifications in just thirteen years. . . . Now they [engineers] would have to build the equivalent of 410 Pennsylvania Turn-pikes, 16,000 exits and entrances, nearly 55,000 bridges and overpasses, and scores of tunnels. They were to build these

Interstates in sparsely populated places where the citizens had little or no experience with limited-access highways. Since 75 percent of the Interstates would be constructed on new right-of-way, they would have to take more land by eminent domain than had been taken in the entire history of road building in the United States. Plans called for them to build through many miles in hostile and rugged territory, places where engineers before them had found it difficult to blaze a dirt trail, much less a four-lane superhighway.

The National System of Interstate and Defense Highways was a daunting task for federal officials, state highway representatives, and road engineers. Yet it was a quintessentially American challenge: big, brash, proud, against the odds, and in need of superhuman amounts of grit and determination. Far from becoming paralyzed by the enormity and difficulty of what needed to be done, all parties rose to the occasion and got to work.

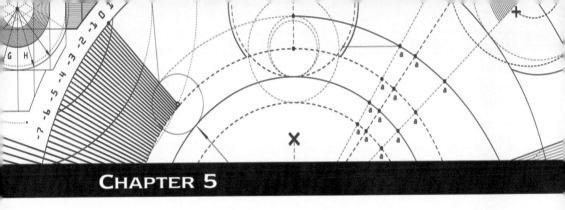

CHAPTER 5

Building the Interstates

Immediately after President Eisenhower signed the Federal-Aid Highway Act of 1956 into law, the Bureau of Public Roads and state highway officials swung into action to plan the highway building that would consume them for the next two decades and beyond. Even as contracts were signed and work was scheduled to begin within six weeks for the first stretches of the Interstate Highway System in Kansas and Missouri, agreements needed to be made concerning construction and design standards. Uniformity of design and engineering was required according to the terms of the new law, as were the highest standards and quality of materials available.

GATHERING DATA

While congressional debates raged over Eisenhower's Grand Plan during 1955 and 1956, the Bureau of Public Roads operated on the assumption that an interstate highway bill would eventually be passed. So, continuing its tradition of federal-state cooperation instituted by Thomas MacDonald, it worked in conjunction with the American Association of State Highway Officials (AASHO) to establish construction and design standards for the future interstates.

The first step was to test various construction methods and materials before deciding on uniform standards for the entire interstate system. The Bureau of Public Roads, AASHO, the Department of Defense, the Automobile Manufacturers Association, the American Petroleum Institute, the American Institute of Steel Construction, and various construction materials manufacturers and transportation associations pooled their resources and funded the building of a seven-mile-long, two-lane test highway in Ottawa, Illinois. The oval-shaped road was divided into 836 test segments; each had a different ratio of asphalt and concrete and varying thicknesses of the road's surface, base, and subbase layers. Some stretches were built using stones, clays, and sand from regions around the country so individual states could see how their locally built stretches of interstate would fare. In addition, sixteen short bridges and six looping sections—to simulate overpasses and exits/entrances—were built.

The Ottawa road was opened to test traffic in mid-October 1956. For the next two years, Department of Defense drivers (usually soldiers) in vehicles both light and heavy (ranging from 1 to 24 tons) drove up and down the road, simulating the heavy, punishing, and constant traffic the new interstates could expect. Some of the 836 stretches were torn to shreds or buckled; others held fast. Reams of data were meticulously collected concerning the performance of various kinds and combinations of materials under the stresses imposed by traffic, weather, and time. The AASHO published this raw data in manuals, which the individual states then used to make decisions about the best engineering strategies to employ, given their local materials, climate, and traffic volume and patterns. The straight stretch of the test road was later incorporated into Interstate 80.

THE BASIC BLUEPRINT

Though states were given freedom of choice over the methods and materials they would use to build their stretches of interstate, uniformity prevailed in other aspects of design. The highways would have limited access, meaning no intersections, railroad crossings, stop signs, or traffic lights would be included (except in a handful of low-traffic rural areas, where at-grade crossings were permitted so that local roads could intersect with and cut across the interstate). To get on the highway, a driver would have to enter at a designated on-ramp and merge with the traffic flow. Similarly, he or she would get off by exiting at a designated spot. Bridges and overpasses would be built to accommodate the older local roads and highways that the new interstates crossed but did not allow access to. These older roads (often the old federal-state highways) would run above, below, or alongside the interstates.

A minimum of two lanes would run in each direction. The highways would be divided: A strip of land or a guardrail would separate the two lanes that ran in one direction from the two lanes that ran in the opposite direction. These median dividers had to be at least 36 feet wide in rural areas and at least 16 feet wide in urban areas. Each lane would be 12 feet wide and designed to accommodate speeds between 50 and 70 miles per hour (mph)—50 mph in mountains, 60 mph in hilly country, and 70 mph on flat stretches. The right shoulder of an interstate would be paved and 10 feet wide. The left shoulder would be 4-foot-wide pavement. At a minimum, tunnels and bridges would allow clearance of vehicles that were 14 feet tall. One hundred feet of land that extended to either side of the highway would be seized by the state government and kept for future use. This was the "right-of-way," and it allowed planners to someday put in utilities, rest areas, and services, or to expand and widen the road to three or more lanes in each direction if traffic volume eventually demanded it.

The Ottawa road *(above)* was an experiment designed by the American Association of State Highway Officials to help determine the best methods of construction for the new interstate roads. Conducted over a period of two years, the project recorded the results of wear and tear on stretches of road that were paved in different ways.

Initially, any given stretch of U.S. interstate was to be designed to accommodate expected traffic volume and wear and tear through 1975. As time went on, the requirement became that any new, upgraded, or repaired stretch of interstate would be designed to accommodate 20 years of use (and abuse). Additional lanes to existing interstates could be built, but they could not be paid for from the Highway Trust Fund. The addition of exits and entrances to an existing interstate would require federal approval.

ESTABLISHING NEW STANDARDS

The design of uniform interstate highway signs and route numbering also had to be established. Once again, the Bureau of Public Roads and AASHO got together and hammered out agreements after lengthy debates. Echoing the black-on-white route number shields that had been adopted as standard by federal-aid highways in the 1920s, the new interstate routes would also be identified by a shield, though these would be red, white, and blue. The blue shield would be topped by a red band, upon which would appear the word "INTERSTATE" in white letters. The route number would appear in white within the blue shield.

Choosing the color of exit signs proved to be surprisingly controversial. Both the AASHO and the Bureau of Public Roads favored green signs with white lettering that would be clearly readable from a distance of 800 feet (almost 300 yards). Yet Bertram Tallamy, the recently appointed federal highway administrator—a position created in 1956 by President Eisenhower to oversee federal highway policy and the interstate program—insisted on blue signs, which he had used when he helped to build the New York State Thruway as a member of the New York State Public Works Department. Still others suggested black signs with white lettering.

To resolve the dispute, the Bureau of Public Roads built another test road. This one, in Greenbelt, Maryland, was only three miles long. At each mile was posted a sign for "Metropolis, Utopia"—one in blue, one in black, and one in green. After driving the length of the test road at 65 mph, hundreds of volunteer drivers were polled concerning their sign preferences. Almost two out of three drivers found the green sign to be most legible from a distance and at highway speed. The white-on-green signs were chosen as the interstate standard. It later became known that Tallamy suffered from color blindness and saw the green signs as a pale yellow. His blue signs made it to the interstates as well; they were used to notify drivers of upcoming rest areas and gas stations.

The AASHO next turned its attention to route numbering. Rather than reinvent the wheel, it decided to stick to the same basic scheme developed for the federal-aid highways in the

BUILDING AMERICA NOW

SUPERPAVE

Following the passage of the Federal-Aid Highway Act of 1956 and the creation of the Interstate Highway System, engineers immediately began testing various road surfaces and combinations of surfacing materials at a test highway in Ottawa, Illinois. Different ratios of asphalt and concrete and varying thicknesses of the road's surface, base, and subbase layers were tested to determine which combination of surfacing held up best under various punishing conditions. In addition, stones, clays, and sand from regions around the country were included in the mixes to determine how specific localities could best use the construction materials they had close at hand.

Similar but far more advanced research on and testing of road surfaces continues today with the federally financed Superpave program. Superpave stands for SUperior PERforming asphalt PAVEments. The program seeks to investigate why some pavements perform well and others do not; develop tests and specifications for materials that will outperform and outlast the pavements constructed today; work with highway agencies and industry to put the new specifications to use; and create durable, longer-lasting, low-maintenance pavements that can withstand extremes of temperature and heavy traffic.

One of the program's other main goals is to test a variety of asphalt mixes and application procedures and to come up with specific combinations and techniques that work best for particular regions and localities. One kind of asphalt does not suit all regions, which differ greatly in terms of average temperatures, typical daily temperature swings, precipitation, humidity, and traffic volume.

1920s. The routes would still be numbered rather than named. East-west routes remained even numbers, and north-south routes were odd numbers. The one change to the system that the AASHO introduced was both brilliant and necessary. It inverted the old system of numbering so that the interstate numbers would increase from west to east and from south to north. Thus, Interstate 5 would run the length of the West Coast, and Interstate 95 would hug the East Coast. I-10 would run from Florida to California, and I-90 would barrel from Massachusetts to Washington State. This flip-flopping of route numbers would prevent confusion between a new interstate and an old U.S. route (a federal-aid highway) that shared the same number and ran near each other in the same state. In addition, major east-west routes would end with a zero, and major north-south routes would end with a 1 or 5. That is why there is no Interstate 1, for example. Interstate numbers would have one or two digits, though urban beltways and spurs could have three digits. Beltways, which bypass (go around) cities, would begin with an even number. Spurs, which flow directly into, through, and out of cities, would begin with an odd number.

Exits were numbered in one of two ways. They could simply be numbered consecutively (exit 1, exit 2, exit 3, etc.), beginning with each interstate's most southerly or westerly exit in a particular state, or they could be numbered according to mileage (if a state's first interstate exit occurred five miles from its most southerly or westerly origin—at milepost zero—it would be exit 5). The next exit, two miles farther east or north down the highway, would be exit 7.

A "FURIOUS PACE"

The first new construction to begin on the Interstate Highway System was on what would become Interstate 70 in St. Charles County, Missouri (the former Mark Twain Expressway segment of U.S. 40). The first shovelful of dirt was tossed from the emerging roadbed on August 2, 1956. The first eight-mile segment of new interstate to be completed was also part of Interstate 70, stretching from Valencia to Maple Hill Corner, just to the west of Topeka, Kansas. It was completed in late September 1956 and officially opened on November 14.

Work on the National System of Interstate and Defense Highways had officially begun, and road engineers and state highway officials were fast out of the gates. Within less than a year from the first groundbreaking in Missouri, the Bureau of Public Roads had approved 80 percent (or about 32,800 miles of the system's 41,000 total miles) of the highway locations selected by states. The states had also set about upgrading and converting almost a thousand miles of older, existing federal-aid highways that would be incorporated into the Interstate Highway System.

Layers of gravel, asphalt, and concrete are poured into a cleared path to create a new road for the interstate system (above). Although some areas required slight adjustments due to climate or terrain, stretches of road were quickly completed in a little more than a month.

More than 2,000 miles of immediately usable highway were added to the Interstate Highway System with the incorporation of several states' existing turnpikes. These superhighways, built in the late 1930s and 1940s, were permitted to continue charging tolls, despite the fact that the interstates were supposed to be primarily freeways, funded by user taxes on vehicle-related products like gas, rubber, and oil. This is why the Pennsylvania Turnpike is now part of Interstates 76, 70, and 276 (and someday will form a part of I-95 if current construction plans proceed) and why the New York State Thruway forms parts of Interstates 87, 287, 90, 84, and 190. Indeed, the Bureau of Public Roads was able to report in 1957, the first full year of interstate building, that planning and construction were moving forward at a "furious pace."

The first five years of this massive building project were mostly consumed with creating roads where there were none before, through farms, fields, forests, plains, deserts, and inner cities. First, engineers flew over a region and photographed the surrounding natural and human-made topography. By studying the photographs, they were able to plot the most simple and straight path for a given stretch of interstate. The interstates were supposed to connect regional cities in as short a distance as possible, on as straight a road as possible, and as inexpensively as possible—even if that meant bridging rivers, tunneling through mountains, crossing over other two-lane highways, or plowing right through someone's home or business. Owners of homes, businesses, and land would have to be paid by the state for their property at "fair market value."

HUMBLE ACHIEVEMENTS ON AN AWE-INSPIRING SCALE

Land had to be acquired, cleared, staked out, and paved. This was an incredibly arduous process, involving both the brute strength of gargantuan earth-moving machines and the carefully calibrated finesse of keen-eyed road engineers. It is estimated that 42 billion cubic yards of earth had to be removed to create the roadbeds that support today's Interstate Highway System. An army of diesel-spewing mechanized scrapers, excavators, bulldozers, dump trucks, and wood chippers, not to mention ordinary men armed only with axes, shovels, saws, and chain-saws, fanned out nationwide to clear woods, strip topsoil, flatten terrain, tunnel through mountains, bridge rivers, and, most importantly, move 100 tons of earth with each scraped and bull-dozed load.

The enormous quantities of earth that were scraped and bull-dozed to clear the land through which the interstates would traverse were, in turn, used to create the highways' roadbeds. Once a channel or path had been created, with embankments placed on each side and water drainage pipes underlying it, the dirt that had been removed to create the channel was reused to form the roadbed. Upon this roadbed was poured a layer of gravel stones, which formed the subbase or foundation of the highway. A thin layer of hot liquid asphalt was poured over this, creating a kind of waterproofing that would protect the road's foundation and prevent the cracking, buckling, heaving, and potholing that occurs when water seeps under the road surface and then repeatedly freezes and thaws. The final layer was the base, made of concrete poured around interconnected, grid-like steel reinforcement bars. In parts of the country that experienced harsh winters, subfreezing temperatures, and/or heavy traffic, roads would have to be built deeper—sometimes as much as five feet deep—and involve several subsurface layers of sand and gravel, coarse gravel, and crushed gravel. More temperate, warm weather areas that saw light traffic might have roadways that were only one foot deep from foundation to surface layer.

The freshly poured concrete required a month to settle and dry. Then the necessary solid and dotted lane and shoulder lines were painted. Exit signs, mileposts, and other highway markers were put in place, and landscape engineers planted trees, flowers, and plants in the median and on either side of the highway. Once work was completed, the stretch of highway was ready to be officially opened to an often impatiently waiting driving public.

The planning was done by unassuming engineers who followed rigid guidelines, and the labor was carried out by legions of anonymous workers. Most of the construction was straightforward, unglamorous grunt work, awe inspiring only in the raw force and energy expended. As quoted by Tom Lewis:

> If highway construction seemed more ordinary than most engineering projects, that's because it was. Much of the building of the Interstate demanded little ongoing engineering imagination. Since the days of the Pennsylvania Turnpike, engineers had known they could build roads that would allow cars and trucks to travel fast safely. . . . Beginning with the Pennsylvania Turnpike construction in 1940, engineers had standardized highway construction—mile after mile of divided roadway with lanes twelve feet wide; ten-foot breakdown lanes; curves and grades that allowed for speeds of seventy miles per hour. The Bureau of Public Roads and the American Association of State Highway Officials issued specifications for construction that left little leeway for interpretation. Engineers simply applied the rules to the task at hand be it Interstate 10 through Santa Monica, California, or Interstate 94 through Dickinson, North Dakota. They simply repeated the tasks in small increments of usually five, ten, twenty, or thirty miles many times over; surveying, walking the line, grading the land, laying the substrate, laying the asphalt or concrete, painting the lines, erecting the signs, holding the ribbon-cutting ceremony, and moving on.

The sheer scale, extent, and doggedness of the building project were more impressive than any particular engineering feats that went into it. Yet, due to the rugged and varied topography of the United States, extraordinary engineering efforts were occasionally required for the interstates to bridge and tunnel their way across America.

Mountains and hilly terrain were a challenge for highway engineers, as tunnels, like the one above in Pennsylvania, would have to be built in order to continue road construction. One of the largest tunnels in the interstate system, the Eisenhower Memorial Tunnel, cuts through the Rocky Mountains and connects western and eastern Colorado.

ENGINEERING MARVELS

Chief among these engineering marvels is the tunnel that would come to bear the name of the Grand Plan's author: Dwight Eisenhower. This tunnel would blast straight through the Rockies and connect eastern Colorado with western Colorado, which, in the wintertime, was often impossible to do. Interstate 70 would now be able to extend west from Boulder, across the Continental Divide, to Grand Junction and points west, all the way to Cove Fort, Utah.

The tunnel would be the highest vehicle tunnel in the world—reaching more than 11,000 feet above sea level—and the very highest point along the entire Interstate Highway System. It actually required the dynamiting and drilling of two tunnels. The first would provide engineers with the geological information they needed to complete the job safely and efficiently; the second would initially serve traffic running in both directions, one lane each way. Once it was completed, crews would return to the first "test" tunnel, widen it, and create a second finished tunnel. Westbound and eastbound traffic would each have their own two-lane tunnel through which they could cross the previously impassable stretch of Rockies at highway speed.

Thousand of workers labored for several million hours for almost 10 years to complete the first operational vehicle tunnel, which, when it opened in 1973, was named the Eisenhower Memorial Tunnel. The second tunnel was finished in 1979. The cost of the project was $125 million—250 percent more than estimated—and nine laborers lost their lives during the building. Yet, having conquered a notoriously treacherous stretch of mountain range, it is now considered one of the safest roads in the world, and one of the greatest road-building achievements.

One of the world's most unique bridges can be found on Interstate 90 in Washington State. This bridge, which connects Seattle with Mercer Island and suburbs beyond, passes over Lake Washington. This lake is too deep (400 feet of water and shifting silt) to allow for traditional bridge support structures, so the bridge actually floats. The roadway is supported by floating concrete pontoons that are attached to cables affixed to the lake bed.

The Fort McHenry Tunnel in Baltimore, Maryland, is the longest and widest underwater highway tunnel ever built by the immersed-tube method, in which a trench is dug in the earth beneath the water and sections of tunnel are inserted into it. The tunnel, part of Interstate 95, is 1.75 miles long. Because it goes under Baltimore Harbor, the tunnel helped to save Fort McHenry—a site made famous by Francis Scott Key's song "The Star-Spangled Banner," which celebrated the fort's survival of a British bombardment during the War of 1812. The original plan for this stretch of I-95 called for a bridge instead of a tunnel. Protestors, alarmed by the prospect of the fort being desecrated by highway noise and exhaust successfully sought revisions to the plan. The state-of-the-art tunnel opened in 1986.

The following year saw the opening of the spectacular Sunshine Skyway Bridge, part of I-275 that connects St. Petersburg and Bradenton, Florida. Almost six miles in length, it is the world's largest cable-stayed concrete bridge. Unlike most suspension bridges, these bright yellow cables support the center of the structure rather than its sides, so drivers and passengers have an unobstructed view of the water when they look to their right.

The Interstate Highway System includes 104 tunnels and 54,663 bridges. Some offer spectacular views or eye-catching designs, but most are rather ordinary, bridging small bodies of water or boring through unexceptional mounds of rock. Yet the interstates could not exist without them. Though they may not be dazzling wonders of the world or innovative engineering breakthroughs, these usually modest structures do the hard work needed to extend the highways throughout the 50 states and keep American drivers moving forward safely.

According to Dan McNichol, author of *The Roads That Built America*, the Interstate Highway System ultimately required more than a billion pounds of dynamite (to blast around and through mountains and to reshape problematic natural contours

Eighty-fourth Congress of the United States of America

AT THE SECOND SESSION

Begun and held at the City of Washington on Tuesday, the third day of January, one thousand nine hundred and fifty-six

An Act

To amend and supplement the Federal-Aid Road Act approved July 11, 1916, to authorize appropriations for continuing the construction of highways; to amend the Internal Revenue Code of 1954 to provide additional revenue from the taxes on motor fuel, tires, and trucks and buses; and for other purposes.

Be it enacted by the Senate and House of Representatives of the United States of America in Congress assembled,

TITLE I—FEDERAL-AID HIGHWAY ACT OF 1956

SEC. 101. SHORT TITLE FOR TITLE I.
This title may be cited as the "Federal-Aid Highway Act of 1956".

SEC. 102. FEDERAL-AID HIGHWAYS.
(a) (1) AUTHORIZATION OF APPROPRIATIONS.—For the purpose of carrying out the provisions of the Federal-Aid Road Act approved July 11, 1916 (39 Stat. 355), and all Acts amendatory thereof and supplementary thereto, there is hereby authorized to be appropriated for the fiscal year ending June 30, 1957, $125,000,000 in addition to any sums heretofore authorized for such fiscal year; the sum of $850,000,000 for the fiscal year ending June 30, 1958; and the sum of $875,000,000 for the fiscal year ending June 30, 1959. The sums herein authorized for each fiscal year shall be available for expenditure as follows:
(A) 45 per centum for projects on the Federal-aid primary highway system.
(B) 30 per centum for projects on the Federal-aid secondary highway system.
(C) 25 per centum for projects on extensions of these systems within urban areas.
(2) APPORTIONMENTS.—The sums authorized by this section shall be apportioned among the several States in the manner now provided by law and in accordance with the formulas set forth in section 4 of the Federal-Aid Highway Act of 1944, approved December 20, 1944 (58 Stat. 838): *Provided,* That the additional amount herein authorized for the fiscal year ending June 30, 1957, shall be apportioned immediately upon enactment of this Act.
(b) AVAILABILITY FOR EXPENDITURE.—Any sums apportioned to any State under this section shall be available for expenditure in that State for two years after the close of the fiscal year for which such sums are authorized, and any amounts so apportioned remaining unexpended at the end of such period shall lapse: *Provided,* That such funds shall be deemed to have been expended if a sum equal to the total of the sums herein and heretofore apportioned to the State is covered by formal agreements with the Secretary of Commerce for construction, reconstruction, or improvement of specific projects as provided in this title and prior Acts: *Provided further,* That in the case of those sums heretofore, herein, or hereafter apportioned to any State for projects on the Federal-aid secondary highway system, the Secretary of Commerce may, upon the request of any State, discharge his responsibility relative to the plans, specifications, estimates, surveys, contract awards, design, inspection, and construction of such secondary road projects by his receiving and approving a certified statement by the State highway department setting forth that the plans, design, and construction for such projects are in accord with the standards and procedures of such State applicable

In 1956, the U.S. Senate and Congress passed the National Interstate and Defense Highways Act *(above)*, a bill that fueled a construction boom in the United States.

and terrains), 3 million feet of wood, almost 2.5 billion tons of cement and gravel, and millions of miles of steel reinforcement bars (thousands of miles of these bars were needed for a single mile of paved interstate). On average, each mile of interstate cost about $1 million to build; some rural stretches cost less than a half million dollars per mile, whereas some urban routes required more than $12 million per mile.

The highway-building business was booming. By the end of 1957, the states had spent more than $4.5 billion on highway development (including interstates and primary and secondary roads). Together, the federal and state governments had already devoted $1 billion of funds to pending interstate projects, and almost a quarter of a billion dollars had been spent on interstate projects that had already been completed.

Trouble was brewing on the horizon, however. After a torrid start, construction supplies were about to dry up, as was the pool of experienced road engineers. Finances would become extremely tight and prompt a full-scale funding crisis. Once the earthmovers and concrete pourers and road pavers began to emerge from rural areas and encroach on the city limits, seeking passage directly through urban neighborhoods, popular anger and occasional revolt suddenly cast the Interstate Highway System in an unfavorable—even sinister—light. The interstate honeymoon was coming to an end.

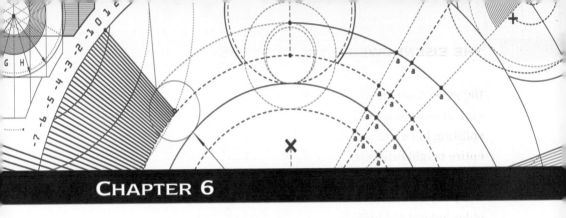

CHAPTER 6

Interstate Controversy and Crisis

As the pace of highway building increased in the years after 1956, the materials needed to build the interstates—such as steel for the reinforcement bars and guardrails, and sand and cement for the concrete surfacing—began to become more and more scarce and expensive. The available pool of engineers required to oversee the massive building project proved to be inadequate. As a result, delays and higher costs began to bedevil Eisenhower's highway system.

Far more troubling, however, was a shift in public attitudes toward the project. Construction delays, detours, and traffic jams quickly soured the mood of Americans who had been promised deliverance from such driving headaches through the building of the Interstate Highway System. Rural Americans became increasingly perturbed by the system's design. Given how wide open their spaces were and how lightly traveled many of their highways were, they could not see the need for four-lane superhighways or a series of expensive, labor-intensive overpasses. They were also increasingly outraged by right-of-way issues and the government's seizure of property to accommodate roadbeds and surrounding buffer land, especially when this required the splitting in two of someone's farm or ranch or the destruction of entire neighborhoods.

The limited-access nature of the superhighways, however, was the element that truly angered many rural residents. The older federal-aid highways—problematic though they were—ran through towns and villages, connecting localities and drawing people into the commercial districts of small towns whose economic health and cultural vitality depended on this kind of traffic. The new interstates largely bypassed these small towns and provided no exits to them or entrances from them. These citizens would have to drive many miles just to gain access to the superhighway, whereas the older highways were designed to pass through where they lived, worked, and shopped. All of this resulted in the death of Main Street businesses, dwindling local populations, and the eventual disappearance of entire towns.

URBAN INTERSTATES

Rural Americans were not the only ones increasingly troubled and even alarmed by the developing Interstate Highway System. Urban Americans also began to view new superhighways as a dangerous encroachment that threatened their businesses, their neighborhoods, their homes, their local culture, and even their health. Initially, Eisenhower's Grand Plan had envisioned a superhighway system that connected American cities but did not pass through them. Urban expressways, beltways, and feeder routes would do the work of funneling traffic into and out of cities. These, in turn, would link up with the interstates, which would be free of the congestion and overabundance of exits and entrances that clog traffic.

What Eisenhower did not know, however, was that his own Bureau of Public Roads had quietly altered his Grand Plan to gain the congressional support it needed to finally pass into law. Though Eisenhower had conceived of an Interstate Highway

System that would link cities and states and primarily traverse rural and suburban areas, politicians were more interested in intracity highways—roads that would pass directly through downtown areas and bring commerce, workers, tourists, and consumers into city areas that had begun to decline.

Because of the postwar suburbanization boom, cities were losing their upper- and middle-class populations and businesses, as well as their substantial tax dollars. As a result of a depleted tax base, city services (such as policing, public transportation, social services, and sanitation) were cut back, creating further flight from urban areas and increased poverty and crime. Many American cities were seriously ailing, even dying, as slums began to move into formerly middle-class neighborhoods. Congressional representatives saw intracity highways—financed primarily by the federal government—as a cheap and effective way to bring people and businesses back to blighted urban areas, revitalize downtown cores, upgrade urban infrastructure, and create jobs.

Sensing this opportunity to gain much-needed support for Eisenhower's foundering plan, the Bureau of Public Roads published and distributed to every congressperson a directory of the urban interstate highways that it proposed to construct through 122 cities in 43 states, each with numerous exits and entrances to facilitate convenient intracity movement. This was known as the Yellow Book, and, given its promises of hundreds of miles of urban highways and billions of dollars of federal funding, it is generally credited with being the decisive factor in gaining the necessary congressional and state support for the passage of the Interstate Highway Act of 1956.

ALTERING THE GRAND PLAN AND DESTROYING NEIGHBORHOODS

Several years after the passage of the 1956 interstate bill, massive highway construction projects began in major American cities, creating even more congestion in city streets and surrounding approach roads that were already clogged by the ever-increasing number of cars on American roadways. In a widely repeated anecdote, Eisenhower is said to have learned of the major intracity highway building going on all around him only when he himself got stuck in a traffic jam in Washington, D.C. When he discovered that the reason for the congestion was the construction of an interstate through a D.C. suburb, he belatedly began to ask his highway officials the hard questions he failed to ask when they drafted the interstate highway bill and pushed for its passage.

The answers Eisenhower received did not please him. Though it was designed partially for defense purposes, the Interstate Highway System was in fact inadequate for defense needs. Its overpasses and bridges were being built three feet shorter than necessary for the safe transportation of missiles and other weapons. Intracity highways served no purpose from a military and defense standpoint: Troops and evacuees needed to move quickly between—not within—population centers. In addition, urban highway building proved to be a massive drain on the Highway Trust Fund. Though urban interstates represented only one-eighth of the system's total mileage, they accounted for half of the system's construction costs. Eisenhower, not known for his interest in the growing plight of American cities, did not understand why the federal government should pay 90 percent of the costs of roadways that benefited only urban localities. In addition, the numerous exits and entrances along intracity routes violated the whole principle and goal of limited-access highways: to move traffic quickly and efficiently between and around cities, with a minimum of interruptions to the steady flow of cars and trucks.

Finally, the urban interstates were being constructed with little to no regard for local concerns, urban planning, or an integrated approach to other forms of transportation, such as commuter trains, subways, and city buses. Local politicians, who knew this was a clumsy and potentially destructive way to address transportation needs and urban renewal, nevertheless felt they had no other choice. As quoted by Tom Lewis:

> Desperate for any federal help, the mayors had chosen to sell the souls of their cities for the jobs and temporary boost to the economy that Interstate highway construction brought. But the price federal and state highway planners exacted for those jobs was enormous. Each mile of [urban] freeway took twenty-four acres of land; each interchange, eighty acres—acres that might otherwise have contributed to the tax structure of a city. All the while the mayors knew their greatest need was for an integrated system of roads and mass transportation, not just Interstate highways tearing through their cities; yet the fear of losing the 90 percent federal share of the financing—the only substantial help the Eisenhower administration had given them—was so great that they chose to deal with the devil.

Instead of analyzing how cities could move people and goods into and out of urban areas through existing infrastructure and forms of public transportation, thereby relieving the need for intracity highways, the interstates were being slapped down—barreling straight through downtown cores and slashing through neighborhoods, regardless of local needs, character, or opposition.

There was, indeed, plenty of local opposition. Urban interstate construction resulted in the razing of entire neighborhoods, most of them poor and many of them populated by minorities. This process became known as "slum clearance." Although highway officials and some local politicians hailed the city interstates as an opportunity to erase unsightly urban blight and revitalize city centers in decline, residents of areas in the path of the highways were displaced, their houses were bulldozed, and their often historic neighborhoods were destroyed, with no traces left behind. Many of these people were then moved into sterile high-rise housing projects that became breeding grounds for crime

Although the interstate system was designed to improve the lives of U.S. citizens, many low income residents were forced to relocate in order to make way for the new superhighways. *Above*, a view of trees in a New Orleans neighborhood before *(top)* and during *(bottom)* interstate construction.

and lacked the communal spirit and vibrancy of their former neighborhoods, impoverished though they were.

In the end, however, Eisenhower—approaching the end of his second and final term as president—decided that it was too late to change direction and restore his original vision of the Interstate Highway System. He could not pull the plug on the urban interstate routes, many of which were already under construction or approaching completion. It would be too embarrassing an admission of error and carelessness, and one that would provoke too intense an outcry among congressional and state representatives. Eisenhower viewed the Interstate Highway System as one of his most valuable achievements, a legacy of monumental importance. He could not turn back now or radically alter what was already under way.

Instead, he simply increased federal funding of the interstate project to help make up for the drain that the intracity highways were putting on the budget. The estimated cost of the entire interstate project had ballooned from $27.5 billion to more than $40 billion, and the Highway Trust Fund was expected to be depleted long before the system was done. Eisenhower, violating his own principle that the system should be self-funded through user taxes, ordered the additional spending of almost $2 billion in federal funds to keep the project on track. He also raised the federal gas tax by one cent, from three cents a gallon to four. Eisenhower did what he felt necessary to save his interstate highways, but it was no longer the system he had envisioned in his Grand Plan.

CORRUPTION, CUT CORNERS, AND CASH SHORTAGES

Following his election to the presidency in 1960, John F. Kennedy was quickly confronted with the ongoing and urgent challenges of the interstate project. By 1961, an additional $11 billion in funding was reported as necessary to complete the Interstate Highway System on time, by 1972. In addition, public support for the project continued to erode as bad press highlighted instances of corruption, including bribery in the awarding of construction contracts, shoddy highway construction, and fraud in the appraisal of land seized for rights-of-way and in the fair valuing of that property and reimbursement to its owners. One investigative journalist referred to the project as "the Great Highway Robbery," and taxpayers' enthusiasm for the increasingly expensive and disruptive undertaking was further dampened. The urban interstates' lack of coordination with the mass transportation systems of the cities they ran through further shook national confidence in the endeavor and cast into doubt the highways' true value.

Though the Interstate Highway System was not President Kennedy's "baby," he responded to the challenges that threatened its future existence with vigor and passion. Confirming Eisenhower's belief in the vital importance of the project, Kennedy reaffirmed the interstates' value from an economic, defense, national security, and driver safety standpoint. As quoted by Richard Weingroff in his article "The Battle of Its Life," President Kennedy proclaimed in a message to Congress that addressed national transportation issues, "An efficient and dynamic transportation system is vital to our domestic economic growth, productivity, and progress. Affecting the cost of every commodity we consume or export, it is equally vital to our ability to compete abroad. It influences both the cost and the flexibility of our defense preparedness, and both the business and recreational opportunities of our citizens." As such, he refused any proposals to either scale back the project or extend its completion schedule.

Instead, Kennedy renewed Eisenhower's one-cent rise in gas taxes, which was about to expire. He also made a number of small changes to similar user taxes that would provide almost $10 billion in additional highway funds during a 10-year period. To better integrate urban interstates with the cities' mass transportation systems and coordinate their efforts, Kennedy

BUILDING AMERICA NOW

THE BIG DIG'S BIG PRICE TAG

During the heyday of interstate highway construction in the late 1950s and 1960s, the average interstate mile cost $1 million to build. A rough average of 2,000 miles of roadway were added annually—through new construction or upgrades of existing roadway—to the system between 1956 and 1970. The intervening years seem only to have made highway projects more costly and time consuming. Boston's ambitious "Big Dig" project—which involved the burying of a stretch of I-93 beneath the city streets—broke ground in 1991. It took more than 15 years to complete the 3.5-mile-long tunnel system. The cost was a staggering $1 billion per mile.

proposed a federal-aid program designed to upgrade older mass transportation systems and create new ones. He also directed the Bureau of Public Roads to engage in more aggressive oversight of the program, granting it new investigative powers that would reduce corruption, fraud, and shoddy construction.

President Kennedy's positive and energetic efforts seemed to address many of the public's growing concerns with the interstate system. Funding was again secure. Corruption in highway planning and construction practices was being rooted out. A more rational and integrated approach to urban highway building was proposed. As a result of this renewed collective confidence in the interstate system and Kennedy's strong advocacy for it, construction again began to proceed with great rapidity. By the end of 1963, almost 17,000 miles of superhighway—more than 40 percent of the system's planned total mileage—had been built and were in operation nationwide.

PAVING OVER LOW-INCOME NEIGHBORHOODS

Other statistics told a very different story, however—one that challenged the equating of the interstates with progress. In the second year of his presidency, Kennedy received a report from his secretary of commerce stating that, every year, 15,000 families and 1,500 businesses were being displaced by interstate construction and right-of-way land seizures. The president ordered that displaced residents and business owners should receive financial assistance and access to other governmental resources to ease their relocation efforts, but these measures proved inadequate to the severe dislocations experienced by urbanites who were transformed into highway refugees.

Although suburbanites generally supported urban interstates to ease their commutes into and out of the city, the people who still lived in the cities—who saw their neighborhoods split in two by an expressway or completely torn down—were understandably outraged. The pittance they received from the government to help them find a new place to live rarely covered their relocation costs and did nothing to restore a lost sense of community, reunite separated neighbors, or preserve a neighborhood's pride and shared history. Anger in the inner cities was building, stoked by the dawning realization that poor and minority neighborhoods were bearing the brunt of the dislocations. Soon, this anger would heat into rage and boil over into all-out revolt.

The residents of low-income urban areas were not mistaken in their suspicion that their neighborhoods were being targeted by the wrecking ball precisely because they were impoverished. The urban interstates did not pass through their neighborhoods simply because it was the most logical route or met the city's most urgent traffic needs. Rather, it all came down to money and influence. Poor neighborhoods were valued lower and therefore required less government compensation to residents and business owners. Poor citizens also held less political power than wealthy campaign donors or angry middle-class voters. Their opinions carried less weight, and their needs and well-being caused less concern.

Chan Rogers, a former Department of Public Works engineer, helped map out the proposed routes of the interstates. As quoted by Dan McNichol, he recalls what the decision-making process was for urban expressways:

> When we were looking for the cheapest place to lay down the Interstates, we would go to the city's tax map that plotted out each lot based on its taxable revenue. Using different colors, we shaded in the high-rent districts in one color and the industrial areas in another and the low-rent districts in a third color. That third color just popped out at you, showing us the cheapest route to build along. The other two areas were avoided because they yielded more tax revenue to city hall. Back then it was all about getting from point A to point B with the least expensive acceptable alternative. Today, we would never be allowed to simply take the course of least resistance and cost. But back then it was perfectly acceptable.

Acceptable, that is, to federal and state planners and city mayors. It was entirely unacceptable to those who lived and worked in the "low-rent districts," though their thoughts were not consulted and their feelings not considered.

PROTESTS RAGE, WITH MIXED RESULTS

Only stubborn resistance would make their wishes finally heard. Indeed, according to Weingroff's "The Battle of Its Life," outcry began to build over the government's apparent policy of building "white men's roads through black men's homes." The needs of suburban drivers were prized over those of inner-city dwellers. Even as billions of dollars were being poured into the interstates—which benefited primarily suburban residents—funds were being cut for the urban mass transportation relied on by most inner-city residents, many of whom did not own cars.

Race riots in Detroit, Michigan *(above)*, were caused by a variety of problems, including construction for the interstate system. Referred to as "urban renewal projects," the government bulldozed poor and minority urban neighborhoods throughout the country in order to make room for new roads.

Class and racial tensions began to seethe in inner-city neighborhoods slated for interstate demolition and construction. These tensions were further intensified during the civil rights struggles of the 1960s and the assassination of civil rights leader Martin Luther King, Jr., following which all-out race riots exploded in cities across America. Many local politicians later blamed these riots in part on the anger and resentment bred by the interstates and their careless, unfeeling, and arrogant destruction of people's homes, businesses, neighborhoods, and communities.

Although poor and often minority inner-city residents had little influence over the interstate decision-making process, another anti-interstate group emerged whose members were generally more affluent, connected, and media savvy. Throughout the 1950s and 1960s, in response to a growing body of scientific evidence that charted humanity's negative effect on the planet's delicate ecological balance, a conservation and environmental movement grew in strength and numbers.

Everything from chemical fertilizers and pesticides to industrial pollution, overdevelopment, and car exhaust suddenly became objects of intense scrutiny for their role in harming Earth's atmosphere and its plants and wildlife. Environmentalists became concerned about the landscapes that were churned up in the wake of the interstates and the effect that the construction and use of these highways would have on soil, streams, animals, and trees. While highway planners simply sought the cheapest and easiest path upon which to lay asphalt, environmentalists began to demand greater care and sensitivity in the choice of locations and the planning of construction.

The political strength of this new environmental movement was proven when, in 1964, the Bureau of Public Roads began requiring state governments to conduct studies of the environmental impact that proposed interstate routes would have on fish and wildlife. In 1965, President Lyndon Johnson (who rose to the presidency following President Kennedy's assassination in 1963) signed the Highway Beautification Act. Johnson was troubled by the fact that every mile of interstate, along with the surrounding right-of-way, essentially destroyed 50 acres of land that could otherwise be parkland and filled it with gas stations, motels, and fast-food restaurants. Yet, he also recognized reality: Cars and trucks were Americans' main form of personal and commercial transportation. They were here to stay. America needed to find a way to better harmonize its car culture with its increasingly fragile environment.

Inspired in part by his wife's complaints about industrial dumps and auto junkyards that lined many highways, Johnson demanded that highways be attractively landscaped, billboards be tightly controlled, junkyards and dumps be screened off by fences or greenery, any land marred by highway construction be restored, and the "beauty and charm" of cities through which highways pass be preserved. As quoted by Weingroff in "The Battle of Its Life," Johnson believed that "highways are for people" and should be designed with the enjoyment of nature and beauty as a first priority; he declared that "highways must be beautiful as seen from the driver's seat . . . and they also must not be a scourge on the community through which they pass."

This first victory against the highway planning forces that valued economic considerations over environmental and community concerns emboldened those who opposed interstate construction in the late 1960s and early 1970s. As the nation became mired in the Vietnam War and various political scandals, distrust of government ran high and protests became a regular feature of daily life. An alliance of anti-interstate interest groups began to emerge, with inner-city activists, environmentalists, and historical preservationists joining forces to protest—and occasionally prevent—the construction of interstate highways through neighborhoods or particularly sensitive natural areas.

Soon, protests were launched against interstate projects in New Orleans, Boston, Philadelphia, New York City, Memphis, San Francisco, Baltimore, and Washington, D.C., among other places. Results were mixed. An elevated highway along San Francisco's waterfront was canceled, as was an expressway in New Orleans that was slated to pass directly through the city's historic Vieux Carre neighborhood in the French Quarter. However, another elevated highway tore through New Orleans' Claiborn Avenue—legendary for both its ancient oak trees and its jazz musician residents—and leveled everything in its path. An expressway that would physically divide a white working-class Baltimore neighborhood from a black one was successfully defeated when the two communities joined forces in resistance. In New York, three massive elevated expressways that were to cut across Manhattan never made it past the drawing board, but in Brooklyn more than 1,500 houses were bulldozed to make way for the Verrazano Bridge and its approaches. Similarly, the Cross Bronx Expressway destroyed huge swaths of neighborhoods throughout New York's largest and poorest borough.

Yet, protestors in Memphis—led by a group of elderly women—were able to save Overton Park, a 342-acre forested recreational area, from planned destruction to make way for Interstate 40. An unusual alliance of ordinarily fractious ethnic neighborhoods in Boston also managed to fight two major interstate projects that would have circled and slashed through its neighborhoods. In this case, I-95 was slated to pass directly through downtown Boston; its elevated beltway, I-695, would ring the downtown area. Eighteen neighborhoods would have been bisected, divided, and cast into concrete and steel shadows by these roadways had local residents not put aside their traditionally volatile class, ethnic, and racial antagonisms to unite in opposition to the plan.

In the end, the threats to neighborhoods and natural areas posed by planned urban interstates often inspired unusual alliances of interest groups from a wide range of racial, ethnic, economic, and political backgrounds. Yet, all in all, poor neighborhoods were far less successful in beating back interstate encroachments, whereas wealthier ones represented by influential advocates were often spared the bulldozer. Race, class, and income level still seemed to determine where a highway was planned, which neighborhood it passed through, and whose homes and businesses it destroyed.

INTERSTATE ACHIEVEMENT AND AGGRAVATION

In 1967, President Johnson created a new cabinet-level federal office, the Department of Transportation (DOT). The Bureau of Public Roads was folded into DOT and became the Federal Highway Administration (FHWA). Through a change of administration—Richard M. Nixon, Eisenhower's former vice president, was elected president in 1968—and ongoing protests, interstate highway building proceeded at a steady clip. By 1970, nearly three-quarters of the Interstate Highway System was complete, with 30,000 miles open to drivers and 5,000 more under construction.

To trumpet its achievements at the dawn of the new decade and in an attempt to dampen anti-interstate sentiment, AASHO issued a celebratory status report on the Interstate Highway System and the benefits it had already delivered. The report

THE INTERSTATE HIGHWAY SYSTEM AT A GLANCE

★ The longest interstate is I-90, which runs 3,020.54 miles from Boston, Massachusetts, to Seattle, Washington.

★ The shortest major interstate is I-97, which runs 16.62 miles from Annapolis to Baltimore, Maryland. Technically it is an intrastate road because it does not leave Maryland.

★ Interstate 80 was the first transcontinental interstate— stretching from the Atlantic to the Pacific—to be fully completed; it opened on August 22, 1986.

★ Texas contains the most interstate mileage: 3,233.45 miles.

★ New York State has the highest number of interstates: 29 routes.

★ There are 104 tunnels and 54,663 bridges throughout the Interstate Highway System.

★ There are more than 1,200 rest areas within the Interstate Highway System and more than 14,000 interchanges (exits and entrances).

★ The northernmost points of the Interstate Highway System are on Interstates 5, 15, and 29, which all end at the Cana-

claimed that travel time between cities had been reduced by 10 percent and that the average speed of travel had increased by more than 10 miles per hour. Both shipping expenses and accident-related costs had decreased dramatically. The report also made sunny but vague claims that the interstates had enriched communities, improved the lives of those displaced by the new highways, and actually reduced air and noise pollution levels.

Facts on the ground belied this cheery assessment, however. Tom Lewis, in his book *Divided Highways*, paints a very different picture of the interstates' effect on American drivers, culture, and the environment:

dian border and the 49th parallel in Washington State, Montana, and North Dakota, respectively. (Alaska's highways do not meet interstate highway standards and are "unsigned" as interstates.)

★ The southernmost points of the Interstate Highway System occur in Honolulu, Hawaii (the 21st parallel), and Miami, Florida (the 25th parallel).

★ The highest point of the Interstate Highway System—11,158 feet above sea level—occurs at the Eisenhower Memorial Tunnel in Colorado on I-70. The lowest point—52 feet below sea level—occurs on I-8 in California.

★ Interstate 95 was the most expensive interstate to build; it cost $8 billion. It is the longest north-south interstate and passes through 16 states, the most of any interstate highway.

★ Interstate highways statistically are twice as safe as any other American roads.

The nation's air—especially in the cities—became more and more clogged with pollution as automobiles burned 130,000 gallons of gas each minute. That year [1970], Americans spent $131 billion for highway transportation and $75 billion for all education programs. . . . One had to look no further than to a medium-sized or large city to see evidence that highways did not move large numbers of people efficiently. In the fifties and sixties, planners . . . responded to the challenge of highway overcrowding by building a new highway or adding lanes to an existing one. New lanes would solve the problem, planners assured everyone. Yet as soon as they were built, the roads acted as powerful magnets that attracted ever more cars and trucks. Planners found that highways designed to meet traffic needs for a decade would be clogged within a year or even a month. As subways deteriorated and trolley lines were abandoned, even more cars entered cities, causing pollution and congestion.

There was no doubt that Eisenhower's vision had been realized in the sense that the Interstate Highway System had allowed the economy to expand. It had led to the dramatic development of both the South and the West, in particular, and had greatly facilitated commerce—in fact, more than 90 percent of the nation's freight was now hauled by trucks that constantly plied the interstate highways. In addition, interstate highways statistically were safer than other American roads. Yet pollution was on the rise, inner cities were dying, and the new superhighways— designed to relieve costly and aggravating congestion—were themselves clogged, despite the billions of dollars spent, the millions of acres sacrificed, and the many thousands of people displaced to make them possible.

Something had to be done to salvage the Grand Plan. It was fitting that Eisenhower's former vice president, Richard Nixon— the man who had formally introduced his boss's interstate plan to the Governors' Conference in 1954—would also be the man to place the highway system on a more solid and sustainable footing. Ironically, Nixon would save the interstates just as their creator finally abandoned the fight. Like George Washington before him, Dwight Eisenhower would not live to see his Grand Plan for a national road network fully realized.

CHAPTER 7

A New Age for the Interstate Highway System

In 1969, the year Dwight Eisenhower died, President Richard Nixon appointed John Volpe to be his secretary of transportation. With his boss's approval, Volpe set out to salvage the Interstate Highway System by, paradoxically, using its trust fund to pay for the development of other forms of mass transportation.

Volpe was alarmed that, as he claimed, more money was spent on highway construction in six weeks than had been spent on urban mass transit in six years. Despite the fact that there was now one mile of interstate highway for every square mile of American territory, these roads were not getting the job done as promised. Reasoning that highways could not bear the entire transportation burden of the nation or its cities, Volpe sought to redirect highway funds to urban mass transit systems, thus creating a more integrated and complementary regional transport system. This is known as intermodal transport, a system in which highways work in conjunction with commuter trains, subways, city buses, and airplanes. When a region's mass transit system is well developed, people can take advantage of convenient and fast alternative transportation, leaving their cars at home and reducing traffic on highways and local streets. Volpe strongly believed that more highways and additional lanes would only intensify the worsening situation, not ease it. Instead, localities had to be consulted and studied to determine what their transportation and community needs actually were and how to best meet them without simply pounding a superhighway through their neighborhoods.

SAVING CITIES, PROTECTING THE ENVIRONMENT, AND LISTENING TO COMMUNITIES

What followed Volpe's appointment were three long years of legislative wrangling and battles with the entrenched highway lobby that had no interest in seeing highway funds redirected or construction slowed (or even halted). Volpe lost the battle in Congress and stepped down as transportation secretary, but his passionate reasoning had strongly affected Nixon.

Following his reelection in 1972, President Nixon indicated that making changes to the Highway Trust Fund would be one of his administration's top priorities. Backed by many of the nation's governors, he proposed granting states the right to designate a portion of the fund to be spent on improvements to their urban mass transit systems. As quoted by Tom Lewis, he warned that, if nothing was done to alter America's current transportation strategy, "our children will grow up in cities which are strangled with traffic, racked by noise, and choked by pollution." Acknowledging the many interstate protests that raged around the country, he said states would now be free to decline spending money on controversial urban highway projects and could instead funnel that money into more useful urban transportation alternatives that would benefit actual city residents and reduce highway- and automobile-related pollution that cast a smoggy pall over America's cities.

Nixon's arguments carried the day after a bruising fight in Congress. By 1975, the Highway Trust Fund was being used not only to pay for Eisenhower's interstates but also to revitalize the transportation systems of America's cities. From this point forward, the Federal Highway Administration would be required to carefully evaluate the social, economic, and environmental effects of a planned highway on the localities it passed through, rather than simply choosing the cheapest path for the road to follow and building it with no regard for the affected communities. The FHWA was also now required to study the transportation alternatives to interstate highways that might better suit local needs. Local officials would designate urban routes.

As part of this process, the FHWA would solicit community input and participation in all project planning and design. It would even ask community members a very basic question: Do you need a highway at all? Those displaced by highway building would begin to receive fair compensation for their homes or suitable replacement housing, and their moving expenses would be paid. In the past, compensation generally was far below the actual value of the property seized, and, if people were relocated at all, they were often placed in less-desirable housing.

Finally, the FHWA, in the tradition of its number-crunching predecessor, the Bureau of Public Roads, launched numerous studies to analyze the impact of interstates on the environment, how to lessen that impact, ways to minimize noise pollution, and how urban traffic affected neighborhood life and community relations. Innovations such as sound barriers, special high-occupancy vehicle lanes for carpoolers, adjacent hiking and bike trails and commuter rail lines, and elaborate landscaping began to be introduced on some interstates.

It was the dawning of a new age for the FHWA and the Interstate Highway System. Humbled by the growing anger they had provoked among American citizens, highway planners, to their credit, learned some hard lessons and began to genuinely try to serve the needs of the public. As the 1970s ended with the

In response to growing environmental concerns and lack of mass transit, Secretary of Transportation John A. Volpe *(above)* proposed to President Richard Nixon a system of intermodal transportation. Designed to provide people with options for alternative transportation such as trains, buses, and subways, Volpe hoped to ease traffic and pollution while providing travel opportunities to those without cars.

country mired in an energy crisis and what President Jimmy Carter labeled a national "crisis of spirit" due to fuel shortages, high gas prices, and economic stagnation, the interstate highways became only one aspect of a much larger national transportation system. The energy crisis, prompted by political turmoil in the oil-rich Middle East, increased the momentum toward greater development of energy-saving mass transportation and intermodal transport. The interstates were no longer the only game in town, and they now had to share the diminishing budgetary wealth.

A QUIET ENDING

As the beleaguered nation limped into the 1980s and began to enjoy an economic renaissance, the interstates had evolved from a much celebrated and appreciated boon, to a widely despised bane, to a simple, ordinary, unnoticed fact of life. By the mid-1980s, the Interstate Highway System was nearly complete, and final stretches of highway were opened with little fanfare or public notice. Interstate 80, the first transcontinental interstate stretching from the Atlantic to the Pacific to be fully completed, opened on August 22, 1986, in Utah. The governor of Utah, the secretary of transportation, and the FHWA chief did not even bother to attend.

What was lost in the midst of all this interstate apathy and antipathy, however, was the fact that, in many important respects, the Interstate Highway System was working exactly as planned and realizing the goals of its creator, Dwight Eisenhower. As quoted by Dan McNichol:

> [T]he Interstate System was expanding Americans' parameters. Families were taking vacations farther and farther from their homes along its ever lengthening routes. The Interstate System was shrinking travel times between cities and suburbs while it was opening parts of the country that were previously unreachable. Businesses continued to take up residence in new office

parks along Interstate highways and beltways, leaving behind the expensive and often run-down cities. By the 1980s, the Interstate System had turned an office, retail, and warehouse boom into a new suburban lifestyle. More workplaces were now located outside of the cities than in them. In the decades since it began, the Interstate System has emerged as the most powerful tool of our domestic economy. It is a rolling horizontal market-place touching every corner of the nation.

Previously remote parts of the country had been opened up to tourism and commerce, especially in the West and the South, where populations had long struggled and local economies stag-nated. Older businesses relocated along interstate corridors, and new ones began alongside them, bringing with them invest-ment and tax dollars and new populations of workers and their families. This, in turn, resulted in the appearance of new shops, services, schools, and suburbs, which meant the making and spending of even more money. Interstate trucking had exploded and was now responsible for the vast majority of commercial goods hauling. Anything purchased by a consumer was probably delivered via an interstate. The economy had vastly expanded thanks to the growing reach of the interstates, just as Eisen-hower had hoped and promised.

END OF THE ROAD?

The Intermodal Surface Transportation Act of 1991 allocated the last of the Highway Trust Fund's resources to a few final con-struction projects, including the last major unfinished interstate segment: Boston's so-called "Big Dig," a rerouting of the formerly elevated I-93 under the city's streets. All future interstate proj-ects would be classified as improvements to the system rather than new construction. The Interstate Highway System, now renamed the Dwight D. Eisenhower System of Interstate and Defense Highways, was, for all intents and purposes, finished at long last.

By the end of 2002, fewer than six miles of the almost 43,000-mile system remained incomplete, with projects in Boston, Massachusetts; Columbus, Ohio; and eastern Pennsylvania either under construction or in the planning stage. A proposed extension of Interstate 69, which runs from the Canadian border with Michigan southeast to Indianapolis, Indiana, would stretch the highway farther south—all the way to Mexico's border with Texas. The future of this project is unclear, as it has met stiff protests from environmentalists and those concerned with the trade and immigration implications the Mexico-to-Canada highway would have.

ONGOING ISSUES AND CONCERNS

The interstates have become a widely accepted, if unloved, part of daily life in America. Few people now argue against their importance or protest their existence, yet they still create controversy and mixed feelings. In an era of increasing anxiety about global warming and resulting climate change, interstates have

CORRIDORS OF THE FUTURE

After an interstate opens, it can still be altered or redesigned. Interstates have continuously evolved, a process that begins the minute after the ribbon-cutting ceremony opens them to drivers. In fact, in 2007, the Department of Transportation named six of the original, most venerable interstates as "Corridors of the Future." These highways—Interstates 95, 70, 15, 5, 10, and 69—together account for nearly a quarter of the nation's daily interstate travel. As part of this new designation, the highways will receive millions of dollars in funding to reduce congestion through the building of new roads, the addition of extra lanes, the opening of truck-only lanes, and the flexible use of lanes that can run in either direction to accommodate shifting traffic demand during morning and evening rush hours.

been blamed for feeding America's addiction to fossil fuels and getting in the way of the development of greener transportation systems, alternative energy sources, and greater use of public transportation.

Sprawl

Suburban sprawl and the emergence of "edge cities" have also been attributed to interstate highways. Although the interstates were created in part to accommodate growing suburbanization, their completion made further suburbanization possible. Housing developments, office complexes, industrial and corporate parks, and strip malls have spread outward from urban areas to fill much of the rural space in between. The delineation between cities and suburbs is increasingly blurred, and suburbs seem to meld into one enormous, endless entity of dense housing and commercial developments. Indeed, more traffic now moves from suburb to suburb rather than from suburb to city, creating new congestion where before there was little. Suburban sprawl has altered the character of America's towns.

Main Street has been replaced by big "box stores," such as Wal-Mart, as well as strip malls and fast-food franchises. Town parks and leafy streets are being replaced by traffic lights, parking lots, "McMansions," and massive shopping centers. This development is also blamed on interstates, which have made longer commutes possible and thus have opened up remote areas to suburban settlement. Many bemoan what they see as the homogenization of the American landscape. They claim that, when a person drives on an interstate, he or she could be anywhere in America; every mile looks almost exactly the same. As the television essayist Charles Kuralt famously observed, "Thanks to the Interstate highway system, it is now possible to cross the country from coast to coast without seeing anything or meeting anybody. If the United States interests you, stay off the Interstates."

Tolls and Privatization

Controversy on the interstates themselves continues to erupt. There is a growing desire among some states to either privatize their interstates (by leasing them to a private, for-profit operator) or charge tolls, or both. The goal is to raise revenue that would help pay for lane additions and maintenance or simply improve the health of state finances.

Though the federal government has traditionally banned tolls on highways paid for by federal money—as the interstates are—it has recently started a pilot program that permits tolls for the purpose of rehabilitating and reconstructing federally financed interstate highways. Tolls are also becoming far easier to collect, without slowing or halting traffic at tollbooths while drivers fumble for cash or toll takers make change. Automatic electronic toll-paying systems such as E-ZPass, FastLane, and SmartTag allow drivers to drive through tolls at highway speed,

BUILDING AMERICA NOW

A NEW INTERSTATE PROJECT, AN OLD DEBATE

Although the Dwight D. Eisenhower System of Interstate and National Defense Highways is officially complete, upgrades and improvements to the system are ongoing. Many of these improvements are small-scale lane additions or short spur roads, but the age of grand interstate projects has not entirely passed—as can be seen with the completion of Boston's Big Dig. A proposed extension of Interstate 69, which currently runs from Port Huron, Michigan, at the Canadian border to Indianapolis, Indiana, would push the highway farther southwest through Illinois, Tennessee, Kentucky, Arkansas, Mississippi, and Texas, all the way to the Mexican border. One thousand six hundred miles of new or upgraded

while an electronic eye scans a device mounted in the car and automatically charges the driver's account.

Yet, as in the days of the early debates over interstate funding, many politicians, policymakers, and ordinary American motorists agree with Thomas MacDonald's passionate belief that public roads must remain public. They argue that American highways must remain open to all Americans, free of charge beyond what is paid through the federal gas tax. The fundamental American freedom of movement should not be privatized and turned into a profit-making business that is less concerned with the safety and convenience of the public it serves than with the money it can make.

Maintenance

As the interstate system ages, and federal and state budgets seem to grow ever tighter, the highways' maintenance has

highway would be added to the interstate system, and I-69 would become the eighth major north-south transcontinental interstate.

This project—a throwback to the ambitious golden age of interstate building, with its massive scale and transcontinental reach—has also brought back the days of anti-interstate protest. Environmentalists, in particular, oppose the plan for the noise and air pollution it would add to a large corridor that currently comprises forest, wetland, and farmland. They argue that the new highway will only add to traffic volume, not lessen congestion, and therefore it will increase the environmental degradation of a huge swath of America. Many people are also concerned with the development that will spring up along the new interstate extension, including suburban sprawl, gas stations, fast-food restaurants, and strip malls.

become a matter of intense concern and sharp debate. The issue was highlighted on August 1, 2007, when an I-35 bridge in Minneapolis collapsed during the evening rush hour and killed 13 people. It soon was revealed that the bridge had been deemed "structurally deficient" in an inspection two years earlier, and that it had shown signs of stress and fatigue, but nothing had been done about it.

In the wake of this tragedy, Americans learned that more than one-quarter of bridges in the country carried loads heavier than they were designed to bear and were categorized by the FHWA as "structurally deficient" or "functionally obsolete." In addition, half of all interstate bridges are more than 30 years old and are approaching the end of their designed life span. Yet a lack of funding prevents proper maintenance and upgrading.

Department of Transportation officials ordered immediate emergency inspections of 700 steel bridges similar to the one that collapsed in Minneapolis, and they promised to review the national bridge inspection program. Without a funding commitment to bridge and other infrastructure upgrades, however, more trouble may be brewing, and tragedy may strike again.

The Big Dig and New Construction

New interstate construction is an equal source of concern. One of the final pieces of the Interstate Highway System—Boston's Big Dig, officially known as the Central Artery/Tunnel Project—was designed to reroute the existing stretch of Interstate 93 (one of the busiest, most congested stretches of interstate in the country) that runs straight through the heart of Boston into a 3.5-mile series of underground tunnels.

The new Central Artery stretch of I-93 zips beneath the city at a depth of as much as 85 feet. Not only does this allow the city to remove the traffic-choked, aboveground elevated highway that cut through downtown, divided neighborhoods, and cut off access to the waterfront, it also allows drivers to pass under the city, avoiding Boston's notoriously tangled streets, jammed traffic, and bewildering interchanges.

The Big Dig, begun in 1991, was a brilliant idea and an engineering marvel. The new roadbed was excavated beneath the old highway, which remained open—the first time in history this had ever been tried, much less achieved. Colonial and Civil War–era artifacts, ships, docks, and pipes were discovered as the new trail was dug out. The tunnel system features 10 lanes and collectively totals 42 miles in length. The tunnel's retaining walls—designed to hold back the waters of Boston Harbor—are the world's largest, as is its ventilation system, which pumps fresh air into the tunnel and pumps out exhaust. The system's exhaust and ventilation fans can generate hurricane-force winds and completely replenish the air throughout the entire tunnel system in only three minutes.

The new underground Central Artery/Tunnel is undeniably awe inspiring. Unfortunately, the project also took more than 15 years and nearly $15 billion to complete. It went over budget by almost $9 billion, while detoured traffic crawled around the construction sites for close to two decades. Despite all the time and money that went into the Big Dig—the most expensive highway project in the history of the United States—serious and troubling problems cropped up immediately.

Shoddy construction practices and poor building materials resulted in thousands of cracks and leaks in the tunnels. Water seepage damaged steel supports and fireproofing systems. Drainage systems were swamped. A July 2006 ceiling collapse resulted in the deaths of two drivers. In the wake of revelations about fraudulent construction practices, lawsuits were launched against various contractors and suppliers who had provided substandard work and inferior materials while pocketing big profits. Several executives of these companies were arrested. Massachusetts is seeking to get back some of the money it paid for this shoddy work, which now must be repaired at still greater expense.

Designed to meet the transportation needs of the population in 1959, the Central Artery highway in Boston soon became clogged with an increasing number of commuters and travelers. A project to move this route underground became known as Boston's Big Dig *(above)* and was one of the last construction projects completed in the Eisenhower Interstate System.

The Big Dig opened some old wounds even as its ambitiousness hearkened back to the glory days of the Interstate Highway System. The disruptive detours, traffic jams, huge expense, and corruption reminded people of what they hated about interstates, while the sheer audacity of the gleaming underground expressway—flawed though it was—reawakened long-dormant visions of an America that dreamed big and built even bigger. It restored, however briefly, a golden vision of the open road, of exhilarating movement through an America knit together by a network of world-class highways.

AN ENDURING MONUMENT TO THE AMERICAN SPIRIT

Aggravation and awe—these are the two poles around which feelings for the Interstate Highway System often gravitate. Often, however, the interstates are "just there"—something most drivers use every day. Nearly 80 percent of all American workers drive to work, and most of them use an interstate to get there. Vehicles travel half a trillion miles on interstates every year. When the roads work well, they receive no praise or attention. When they become clogged with traffic, they are grumbled about and viewed as a necessary evil. Although there is now no real controversy concerning their existence or value, there also is not much lingering sense of that initial awe and pride that greeted the dawn of the interstate age.

In a sense, this may be the most powerful testament to the Interstate Highway System: It has become such an integral part of the American fabric, so essential to our daily lives, that it has entered the hardworking realm of the ordinary. Yet—as with air travel, space exploration, and Internet technology—just because the interstates have become part of our everyday routine does not make their achievement any less awe inspiring. Though the Dwight D. Eisenhower System of Interstate and National Defense Highways is effectively completed, it will continue to evolve to accommodate new technology, new traffic patterns, new vehicles, new environmental realities, and new fuel sources. Its tens of thousands of paved miles, bridges, tunnels, and interchanges—though composed of concrete, asphalt, and steel—are a sort of living organism, the nation's vitally important circulatory system. It will grow and develop right along with the people it works hard to serve and remain a testament to the men and women who conceived of, engineered, and built such a monumental system that lives and breathes.

Just as President Eisenhower envisioned in his Grand Plan, the Interstate Highway System has strengthened our national defense, provided efficient evacuation routes, allowed the

U.S. Interstate Highway System

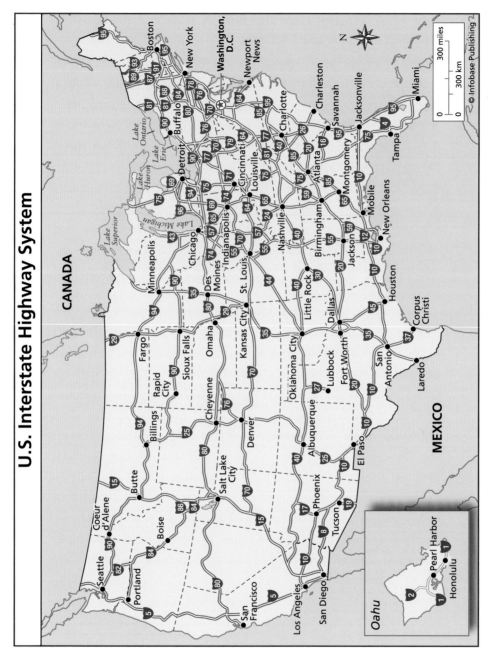

The Eisenhower Interstate System has become the transportation backbone of the United States. By unifying the country through a network of highways, it has created opportunities in commerce, tourism, and travel and continues to grow to meet the needs of the U.S. population.

American economy to greatly expand, increased driver safety, and opened the country to greater development. Most of all, it unified the country—linking town to city, farm to market, state to state, and region to region. The United States became united in more than name only. The Interstate Highway System—planned, designed, engineered, and built by hardworking Americans for the use of all Americans—has itself forged a more perfect union.

1893	Charles and Frank Duryea successfully test-drive their "Buggyaut," a one-cylinder, gasoline-powered horse carriage on wheels; Massachusetts creates the nation's first state highway department.
1894	The federal Office of Road Inquiry is created.
1903	Henry Ford enters the car manufacturing and sales business, offering his Model 999 car to the public; in 1908, he introduces the Model T.
1907	The results of a federal road census reveal that there are only 141 miles of paved rural road in the United States.

TIMELINE

1903
Henry Ford enters the car manufacturing and sales business

1916
The Federal-Aid Road Act funds federal-state highway construction and creates the Bureau of Public Roads (BPR)

1940
The Pennsylvania Turnpike opens

1903 ——————————————— **1954**

1914
The American Association of State Highway Officials (AASHO) is formed

1926
Uniform standards for signage and a rational route numbering system are adopted for the nation's interstate highways

1954
President Eisenhower proposes his Grand Plan for a national Interstate Highway System to the nation's governors

1914   The American Association of State Highway Officials (AASHO) is formed.

1916   The Federal-Aid Road Act funds federal-state highway construction and creates the Bureau of Public Roads (BPR).

1919   Thomas Harris MacDonald is named chief of the BPR. The U.S. Army launches its transcontinental convoy to call attention to the nation's inferior network of roadways.

1922   The Pershing Map is created, identifying the interstate roads most crucial to national defense and security.

1955
An AASHO report claims that travel time between cities has been reduced by 10 percent and that average speed of travel has increased by more than 10 miles per hour

1965
President Lyndon Johnson signs the Highway Beautification Act

1955 1991

1956
Congress passes the Federal-Aid Highway Act of 1956; the first section of interstate highway opens in Kansas in late September

1991
The interstates are renamed the Dwight D. Eisenhower System of Interstate and Defense Highways

1926 Uniform standards for signage and a rational route numbering system are adopted for the nation's interstate highways.

1938 President Roosevelt proposes a system of transcontinental interstate superhighways, running north-south from border to border, and east-west from coast to coast.

1940 The Pennsylvania Turnpike opens.

1944–1945 General Eisenhower creates the "Red Ball Express" and uses French and German highways to ferry troops, artillery, and materials to the European front of World War II.

1953 Thomas MacDonald retires from the BPR, having overseen the paving of 3 million miles of American roadway.

1954 President Eisenhower proposes his Grand Plan for a national Interstate Highway System to the nation's governors.

1955 Interstate construction is in full swing.

1955–1958 Standards are created for building materials, roadway designs and construction, signs, bridge and tunnel construction, and route numbering.

1956 Congress passes the Federal-Aid Highway Act of 1956, creating the National System of Interstate and Defense Highways; the first interstate construction begins in Missouri that summer; the first eight-mile section of interstate is completed and opens in Kansas in late September.

1963 President Kennedy renews Eisenhower's one-cent rise in gas taxes and makes small changes to similar user taxes; he also proposes a federal-aid program to upgrade older mass transportation systems and create new ones.

1964 The BPR requires state governments to conduct studies of the environmental impact proposed interstate routes would have on fish and wildlife.

1965 President Lyndon Johnson signs the Highway Beautification Act.

1967 President Johnson creates a new cabinet-level federal office, the Department of Transportation (DOT). The BPR is folded into DOT and becomes the Federal Highway Administration (FHWA).

1970 Nearly three-quarters of the Interstate Highway System is complete, with 30,000 miles open to drivers and 5,000 more under construction. Still, anti-interstate protests led by neighborhood activists and environmentalists rage throughout America's cities.

1975 The Highway Trust Fund is used not only to pay for interstate construction but also to revitalize the transportation systems of America's cities.

1986 The Interstate Highway System is nearly complete, and final stretches of highway are opened with little fanfare or public notice; Interstate 80, the first transcontinental interstate stretching from the Atlantic to the Pacific to be fully completed, opens on August 22, 1986, in Utah.

1991 The Intermodal Surface Transportation Act allocates funds for highway projects that remain unfinished and officially declares the Interstate Highway System completed; the interstates are renamed the Dwight D. Eisenhower System of Interstate and Defense Highways.

1991–2006 Boston's Big Dig project takes 15 years and almost $15 billion to complete.

2002 Fewer than 6 miles of the almost 43,000-mile system remain uncompleted, with projects in Boston, Massachusetts; Columbus, Ohio; and eastern

Pennsylvania either under construction or in the planning stage.

2006   A ceiling collapse in Boston's I-93 Central Artery/ Tunnel (Big Dig) system results in the deaths of two motorists and reveals hundreds of flaws in the tunnel system as well as incidents of corruption and shoddy workmanship.

2007   An I-35 bridge in Minneapolis collapses during the evening rush hour, killing 13 people; Department of Transportation officials order immediate emergency inspections of 700 steel bridges similar to the one that collapsed in Minneapolis, and it promises to review its national bridge inspection program.

2007–?   An extension of Interstate 69, which currently runs from Port Huron, Michigan, at the Canadian border to Indianapolis, Indiana, is proposed; it would make I-69 the eighth major north-south transcontinental interstate.

GLOSSARY

accessible   Able to be approached or entered easily.

allocate   To set apart and/or distribute something for a specific purpose.

asphalt   A black, tar-like substance mixed with sand and/or gravel to make cement.

beltway   An expressway that passes around an urban area.

bonds   Certificates sold by governments or businesses. The purchaser cashes in these certificates on a certain date and receives the purchasing price plus interest back. The selling of bonds allows governments or businesses to raise a lot of money quickly to pay for important projects.

budget   A plan or schedule of expenses within a given period balanced against expected income or earnings.

cargo   A load of goods or material carried by a car, truck, ship, train, plane, rocket ship, or other vehicle.

commerce   The buying and selling of goods.

concrete   A building material that is made of sand and gravel and is bonded together with cement to make a hard, compact surface.

constituents   The voters represented by a particular public official.

deteriorate   To become worse; to become lower in quality.

eminent domain   The right of a government to seize private property for public use, usually with fair compensation to the owner.

environmental racism   Racial discrimination in the enforcement of environmental rules and regulations; targeting of minority communities for the location of polluting industries; or the exclusion of minority groups from public and private boards, commissions, and regulatory bodies.

expressway   A limited-access, divided highway designed for nonlocal, high-speed through traffic; also known as a superhighway.

federal   Relating to the central government or authority in a union of states; relating to the duties and responsibilities associated with the central government.

freight   Goods that are transported from one place to another.

funding   The providing of money to pay for something.

highway   A public road, open to everyone; a main road or thoroughfare.

homogenization   The process of making things uniform in texture, structure, or appearance; to make things similar or identical.

infrastructure   The basic structures and facilities that make civilized society possible, such as roads, bridges, electrical plants and wires, schools, and communication and transportation systems.

innovation   Something newly introduced; a new method or device; a new way of doing things.

intercity   Between two or more cities.

interstate   Between two or more states.

intracity   Within a city.

intrastate   Within a state.

legislation   The process of making laws; the laws that are made.

lobby   To try to get legislators to vote for a bill you support or against a bill you oppose.

maintenance   Upkeep; the act of keeping something in good working order and good repair.

privatization   The act of transforming a publicly owned institution into one owned by an individual or group of investors who will run the operation with the intention of making a profit.

right-of-way   A strip of private land acquired by the government so that a public road (or railroad, utility, etc.) can be placed on or near it.

shoddy   Poor quality; inferior; poorly done or made.

signage   A system of signs or markers.

sprawl   To spread out in an uneven or unnatural or uncontrolled way; to take up more space than necessary.

spur   A short projecting branch of a larger primary roadway.

transcontinental   Crossing the entire continent; coast to coast.

turnpike   A toll road; usually an expressway that drivers pay to use.

urban blight   A process by which a city, or a part of a city, falls into a state of decay.

visionary   A person whose ideas and plans are fantastic and idealistic; someone who is a dreamer; someone who dreams of things that do not yet exist.

BIBLIOGRAPHY

Broad, William J. "Federal Rules to Improve Design of Highway Bridges Will Go Into Effect in October." *New York Times.* August 4, 2007, section A, p. 11.

"Dwight D. Eisenhower National System of Interstate and Defense Highways." Federal Highway Administration. Available online. http://www.fhwa.dot.gov/programadmin/interstate.cfm.

"Federal Highway Administration Announces $1.59 Million in Grants for Innovative Highway Technologies." Federal Highway Administration. Available online. http://www.dot.gov/affairs/dot12107.htm.

Garreau, Joel. *Edge City: Life on the New Frontier.* New York: Anchor, 1992.

Goddard, Stephen B. *Getting There: The Epic Struggle Between Road and Rail in the American City.* Chicago: University of Chicago Press, 1996.

Gutfreund, Owen D. "Driving Takes Its Toll." *New York Times.* Available online. http://www.nytimes.com/2004/09/04/opinion/04gutfreund.html?_r=1&oref=slogin.

Hamill, Sean D. "Pennsylvania Political War Over Planned Tolls on I-80." *New York Times.* Available online. http://www.nytimes.com/2007/08/26/us/26highway.html.

Lewis, Tom. *Divided Highways: Building the Interstate Highways, Transforming American Life.* New York: Penguin, 1997.

McNichol, Dan. *The Roads That Built America: The Incredible Story of the U.S. Interstate System.* New York: Sterling, 2006.

Mertz, Lee. "The Bragdon Committee." Federal Highway Administration. Available online. http://www.fhwa.dot.gov/infrastructure/bragdon.htm.

Mertz, Lee. "Origins of the Interstate." Federal Highway Administration. Available online. http://www.fhwa.dot.gov/infrastructure/origin.htm.

Mertz, Lee, and Joyce Ritter. "Building the Interstate." Federal Highway Administration. Available online. http://www.fhwa.dot.gov/infrastructure/build.htm.

"The National Highway System." Federal Highway Administration. Available online. http://www.fhwa.dot.gov/hep10/nhs/index.html.

Patton, Phil. "The Virtues of Avoiding Interstates." *New York Times.* August 5, 2007, section 8, p. 11.

"A Partnership for Better Pavements: Making the Promise of Superpave a Reality." Federal Highway Asministration. Available online. http://www.fhwa.dot.gov/pavement/asphalt/regional.cfm.

Rose, Mark H. *Interstate: Express Highway Politics, 1939–1989.* Knoxville: University of Tennessee Press, 1990.

Smothers, Ronald. "New Jersey Set to Expand Turnpike." *New York Times.* Available online. http://www.nytimes.com/2004/12/01/nyregion/01turnpike.html.

Tierney, John. "Life, Liberty, and Open Lanes." *New York Times.* Available online. http://select.nytimes.com/2006/07/01/opinion/01tierney.html.

"U.S. Department of Transportation Names Six Interstate Routes as 'Corridors of the Future' to Help Fight Traffic Congestion." Federal Highway Authority. Available online. http://www.fhwa.dot.gov/pressroom/dot0795.htm.

Wald, Matthew L., and Kenneth Chang. "Hundreds of Inspectors Check Nation's Old Steel Bridges." *New York Times.* August 4, 2007, section A, p. 11.

Weingroff, Richard F. "Along the Interstates: Seeing the Roadside." Federal Highway Administration. Available online. http://www.fhwa.dot.gov/infrastructure/along.cfm.

Weingroff, Richard F. "The Battle of Its Life." *Public Roads* 69, no. 6 (May/June 2006): 26–38.

Weingroff, Richard F. "Essential to the National Interest." *Public Roads* 69, no. 5 (March/April 2006): 47–55.

Weingroff, Richard F. "Original Intent: Purpose of the Interstate System, 1954–1956." Federal Highway Administration. Available online. http://www.fhwa.dot.gov/infrastructure/originalintent.cfm.

Weingroff, Richard F. "The Year of the Interstate." *Public Roads* 69, no. 4 (January/February 2006): 2–11.

Yaffa, Joshua. "The Road to Clarity." *New York Times.* Available online. http://www.nytimes.com/2007/08/12/magazine/12fonts-t.html.

Davidson, Janet F., and Michael S. Sweeney. *On the Move: Transportation and the American Story.* Washington, D.C.: National Geographic, 2003.

Davies, Pete. *American Road: The Story of an Epic Transcontinental Journey at the Dawn of the Motor Age.* New York: Henry Holt & Co., 2002.

Duany, Andres, Elizabeth Plater-Zyberk, and Jeff Speck. *Suburban Nation: The Rise of Sprawl and the Decline of the American Dream.* New York: North Point Press, 2001.

Hokanson, Drake. *The Lincoln Highway: Main Street Across America.* Iowa City: University of Iowa Press, 1999.

Kaszynski, William. *The American Highway: The History and Culture of Roads in the United States.* Jefferson, NC: McFarland & Co., 2000.

Kay, Jane Holtz. *Asphalt Nation: How the Automobile Took Over America and How We Can Take It Back.* Berkeley: University of California Press, 1998.

McNichol, Dan. *The Roads That Built America: The Incredible Story of the U.S. Interstate System.* New York: Sterling, 2006.

Raatma, Lucia. *Dwight D. Eisenhower.* Mankato, MN: Compass Point Books, 2002.

Wallis, Michael. *The Lincoln Highway: Coast to Coast from Times Square to the Golden Gate.* New York: W.W. Norton, 2007.

Wallis, Michael. *Route 66: The Mother Road.* New York: St. Martin's Griffin, 2001.

White, E.B. *Farewell to Model T and from Sea to Shining Sea.* New York: Little Bookroom, 2003.

Witzel, Michael Karl, and Gyvel Young-Witzel. *Legendary Route 66: A Journey Through Time Along America's Mother Road.* Osceola, WI: Voyageur Press, 2007.

Young, Jeff C. *Dwight D. Eisenhower: Soldier and President.* Greensboro, NC: Morgan Reynolds, 2001.

PICTURE CREDITS

INDEX

JOHN MURPHY was born near exit 8A of the New Jersey Turnpike, grew up along the I-95 and U.S. 1 corridors, and spent his formative years driving up and down the length of these venerable highways. He also has made numerous cross-country trips, utilizing three of his favorite interstates—70, 80, and 90. Murphy has a master's degree in Medieval Irish poetry and has survived Ireland's notoriously narrow, treacherous roadways. He loves Ireland deeply, but he'll take the Interstates any day.